£2.95

Lincolnshire Windmills
a contemporary survey

by

Peter Dolman

Published by Lincolnshire County Council: Department of Recreational Services — Museums 1986, with the financial help of the Grants Sub-Committee

Cover picture: Alford Mill, 1985 by Peter Dolman

CONTENTS

1. Introduction 3
2. Windmill Technology and the 'Lincolnshire Windmill' 3
3. Millers and Millwrights 6
4. Preservation and the Future 6
5. About this Survey, and acknowledgements 7
6. Gazetteer of Mills 10
7. Some Bygone Mills 30
8. Map 33
9. Photographs 34
10. Selected Bibliography 64

LINCOLNSHIRE WINDMILLS

by

Peter Dolman

Introduction

Lincolnshire is one of the largest of the English Counties and being mainly level and low-lying is ideal windmill country, forming an extension to the well-known 'Windmill Land' of East Anglia. The total number of windmills to have stood in the county at the peak of the windmill's popularity in the early 19th century can only be guessed at without conducting extensive research; including Fenland pumping windmills there were probably more than 500. Being essentially rural in character with few large industrial towns, the small country windmill was able to hold its own against the large power driven town flour and animal feed mills with the result that Lincolnshire was one of the last areas to use windpower to any extent. A side effect of this is that large numbers of windmills have survived to the present day. This late survival has been aided by the fact that the tower mill, the most durable type of windmill, had become common in Lincolnshire by the early 19th century, whereas in a county such as Suffolk, where post mills and smock mills were more popular, very few mills have survived due to their inability to remain intact without maintenance.

In Lincolnshire today can be found the remains of 136 windmills, only two of which were not corn grinding mills. Of the other English Counties, only Norfolk exceeds this number, but in that county nearly half of the 180-odd mills were marshland pumping mills in the Norfolk Broads. The purpose of this book is to bring the surviving windmill heritage of the county, with its distinctive 'type' to the attention of a wider public. Because of the size of the county and the huge number of windmills once standing in it no attempt has been made to produce a definitive history of all Lincolnshire windmills, such as has been done with some counties in the South and East of England. This would be a life-time's work for anyone and is surely a project worth embarking upon for a local mill historian. The original intention was to produce a straight-forward 'Contemporary Survey' of the mills as they remain, to fit the series of such books produced by Arthur C. Smith and others (see the Bibliography of this book). However, thanks to the excellent 'Lincolnshire Mill Archive' at the Museum of Lincolnshire Life it has been possible to put some flesh on to the bare bones of such a survey, largely based on the notes and research of the late H.E.S. ('Sid') Simmons. Regretably it is apparent that Simmons' notes are rather muddled in some cases and I have therefore attempted to weed out the inaccuracies. I hope the reader will forgive any errors in the historical or technical data; indeed I hope that the sketchy nature of my notes will stimulate further research so that we may eventually gain full appreciation of the special place Lincolnshire's windmills have in the history of windpower.

Windmill Technology and the 'Lincolnshire Windmill'

The Windmill, as found in this country at least, comprises two basic types, the Post Mill and the Tower Mill. In the former type, the whole of the mill machinery is carried in a large timber box-like structure which pivots upon a large oak post, from which the type derives its name. All the earlier mills in Lincolnshire would have been of this type, which normally had the supporting struts for the post (the 'trestle') exposed to the elements on low piers of masonry. By the late 18th century it had become common practice to enclose the trestle in a brick 'round house', which in addition to protecting the trestle from the weather provided extra storage space. Sometimes a conical roof completely enclosed the trestle, but a more frequent type in Lincolnshire was the 'Midlands Roundhouse', which was narrow and usually tapering, with the roof, such as it was, being attached to the bottom of the mill body like a 'skirt'. There was often a curb on top of the wall on which several large rollers ran to help steady the body as it pitched about on the post in a strong wind. The disadvantage of this type of roundhouse was that it was not so spacious, and allowed the vulnerable joints at the ends of the trestle to project outside, where the weather could get at them. Post mills were usually faced into the wind by means of a tailpole and normally had two pairs of millstones, either arranged in the head and tail or both across the head. As only one post mill survives in the county, at Wrawby, I will refrain from a lengthy analysis of post mill design and refer the reader to the section on that mill in the gazetteer for more information.

The tower mill differs from the post mill in that all the machinery is contained within a fixed tower with only the very top, or cap, which carries the sails, turning to face the wind. This means that a very much larger structure could be built, with increased storage space and room for auxiliary machinery. In theory such a mill could contain as many storeys as the builder desired but in practice ten storeys was the usual maximum, with the majority of mills containing between four and seven.

A sub-type of tower mill is the 'smock mill' in which the tower is built of timber instead of brick or stone, and is usually clad with weatherboarding. Smock mills were never very common in Lincolnshire as corn mills, although they were almost universal in the Fenland and other marsh districts where they were employed as drainage mills. A possible source of confusion arises over the term 'smock mill'. I use it in its accepted modern sense of a wooden tower mill; however, in the 18th and 19th centuries it was often local practice to call all tower mills 'smock mills', and the actual building material is not always specified in old sale notices.

The most common building material for tower mills in Lincolnshire is brick, sometimes left unpainted but usually given a coat of tar or occasionally paint to prevent rain from soaking in. In the stone-building areas of the South-West and North one could occasionally find limestone used but it was never very popular and only isolated examples remain as at Hibaldstow, built of rubble walling, and Oasby Mill, Haydor, built of ashlar walling (accurately shaped and coursed stones). Tall mills usually had a stage around the tower about a third of the way up. Originally these would have been wide enough to reach the end of the sails to adjust the cloth or shutters but after patent sails became accepted as standard the stage was relegated to a narrow walk-way just wide enough to adjust the striking weights and operate the brake rope. The railings were sometimes of wood and sometimes of iron. Particularly fine wrought-iron railings can be seen at Huttoft and Sibsey.

The feature most easily recognizable about Lincolnshire mills is the 'ogee' shaped cap. This seems to have become popular at the close of the 18th century and is an exaggerated form of the dome and final type of cap which a few older mills retained. Although all the 'ogee' caps have similar features such as the exposed corners of the cap frame and a prominent sweep up to the finial, there are local variations. In the North of the county caps were often narrow with a vertical 'petticoat' while further south a more 'bulbous' type was favoured with an inward facing petticoat, often meeting the corbelled-out brickwork at the top of the tower where occasionally a decorative 'dog tooth' band is introduced. The cap is constructed with a heavy frame, usually of oak, which runs on a track (called the 'curb') on top of the tower, kept central by a number of centring or 'truck' wheels. The roof is framed very lightly, with radial ribs running up from a cap circle to the central finial and is covered with a double layer of boarding, the inner laid horizontally and flush jointed, with the outer layer of tapered boards laid vertically with a weatherboarded effect to discourage water from penetrating from the front. An application of painted canvas was sometimes used to seal a leaking cap roof. Finials differ from one area to another, some having a short stalk and some a very long one. The terminal ball is often of hollow cast iron but beaten copper ones were also used.

Virtually all the mills to remain have eight-bladed fantails to turn the cap into the wind via reduction gearing to a toothed rack on the curb. The method of turning the cap by hand is rather neatly executed in many mills with a compact cluster of gears inside the cap and a crank handle.

The other feature most associated with Lincolnshire windmills is the use of more than four sails. This practice was adopted widely in the county from the late 18th century onwards, spreading into neighbouring counties, although not to any great extent. At first five sails were tried, which gave a significant boost in power compared with four sails. However the obvious disadvantage is that should a sail be lost or damaged the mill is unable to work until a replacement is fitted. It cannot have been long before six sails were found to be the answer, giving terrific power and at the same time allowing work to continue in the event of damage by juggling the remaining sails around. The ultimate was the eight sail mill, but these never caught on like the five and six sail mills did and only a handful were built. They suffer from the fact that each sail causes turbulence in the wind-flow for the following one and also that the wind will tend to veer around the sails, missing them altogether. They are however particularly well suited to working in lighter winds which is where they scored over four sail mills.

In Lincolnshire, 'Cubitt's Patent Sails' are almost universal. They were invented in 1807 and came into use rapidly due to their ease of control and self-regulating ability. Each sail has a series of shutters, or 'shades' as they are known locally, which are all linked together by a rod, connected via various links and cranks to a central 'spider' coupling mounted on the iron striking rod which passes through the hollow windshaft. The striking rod is connected to a large lever at the back of the cap to which the striking chain is attached, passing down to the stage, or ground and back up to the lever by way of a pulley which enables the lever to be raised or lowered, thus opening or closing the shades. To keep the shades closed against the wind pressure a weight is attached to one side of the chain and if this is carefully adjusted the sails can be made to govern their speed. As a strong gust strikes the mill, the shades blow open, lifting the weight and spilling the wind. When the gust subsides, the weight closes the shades, giving full power once more.

An earlier form of shuttered sail, now only to be found at Wrawby mill, is the 'spring sail'. In this type the shades are balanced against wind pressure by a spring on each sail, which therefore have to be adjusted independently. The oldest type of sail is the 'common sail', in which sail cloth is spread across a lattice framework by hand and tied on. No examples of this type can be found in the county now although they were once popular with smaller mills such as post mills, where they were sometimes run with a pair of spring sails to give some measure of control. Their big drawback was that the mill needed to be stopped while producing full power in order to reef the sails, something that wasn't always possible in sudden squalls. One other type of sail was once common in Lincolnshire, 'Hooper's Roller Reefing Sail'. This type used sailcloth on transverse roller blinds, all the blinds in each sail being connected by a pair of striking rods to a central 'spider', similar to that used with 'patent sails'. These sails were not as good as patent or spring sails for automatic regulation, relying solely on centrifugal force to reef the blinds instead of wind pressure and were also costly and troublesome to maintain. They were once fairly common but no examples can be found in the county now — indeed the only remaining set of such sails are on a mill in Northern Ireland. There were two other forms of 'patent' sails used in isolated cases but these are described later in the gazetteer with their relevant mills.

Mill sails usually run anti-clockwise when viewed from the front ('right-handed'), but some mills were built to run clockwise, as at Burgh-le-Marsh. Shuttered sails can be either double sided, with shades on both sides of the sail 'back', or single sided, with shades on the trailing, or 'drive' side only. The latter form is preferred and is said to work better than the double type, despite having less sail area, due to better aerodynamic performance.

The standard sail fixing in Lincolnshire is to bolt and clamp the sail back onto a cast-iron 'cross' (see illustration p.8) mounted on the windshaft. This type of mounting has so many advantages it is surprising that it was not more widely adopted, being largely confined to the East Midlands, Lincolnshire and the North-East of England. It allows for more than four sails to be used if desired and also means that the maximum length of timber required is around 35 feet instead of over 50 feet for a 'stock'. The older type of sail fixing was to mount each pair of sail frames on a long 'stock' which passes through the 'poll-end' of the windshaft. These were originally all wood but were latterly of iron, or of wood with an iron poll-end. This type of windshaft was sometimes used in the county, but now only one remains, at Lutton.

Mounted on the windshaft is a large wheel of some 8 feet diameter called the 'brakewheel'. This is usually of wood, with four spokes arranged in pairs ('clasp-arm') however cast-iron components such as a hub and arms are sometimes used and later mills often had wheels entirely of iron. Almost all the brakewheels were fitted with iron teeth in the form of segments of a circle, bolted on. Lutton mill retains the older wooden cogs, morticed into the brakewheel. The brake is either built from several segments of wood or is a continuous iron band, fixed at one end to the cap frame and at the other to a lever, which normally holds the brake 'on' by its own weight. A hook is provided to hold the lever up, thereby releasing the brake and a rope and pulleys are provided to operate the brake from the ground, or from the stage.

The brakewheel engages with a wheel on the upright shaft called the 'wallower', which is usually of cast iron, sometimes with wooden cogs as at Burgh le Marsh, or occasionally entirely of wood as at Moulton. The underside of the wallower has a track attached to drive the sackhoist, a wheel being pressed into contact with the revolving wallower to engage the drive. Many mills use an endless chain on the hoist instead of a single chain.

The upright shaft is usually in two or three sections with the upper one connected by a universal joint to allow for any slight eccentricity in the cap. Wood is sometimes used throughout as at Maltby le Marsh, but more often the lower section carrying the great spur wheel is of cast iron and in later mills the whole shaft is entirely of cast iron. There is sometimes a 'crown wheel' on one of the upper floors to drive grain cleaning machinery, as at Alford. On the stone floor can be found the 'great spur wheel' which drives the stones. This is usually entirely of cast iron, with some older mills retaining wooden 'clasp-arm' wheels, although these have mostly had the original wooden cogs replaced by cast iron segments of teeth. The wheel in Moulton mill is of composite construction with an iron hub and rim and wooden cogs and 'compass-arm' (or radial) spokes. The millstones are driven from above by means of a small iron 'stone nut', usually with morticed wooden cogs, mounted on a 'quant' which drives the upper millstone by way of a forked end and a 'mace' coupling. The overall gear ratio is usually about 10:1 so at 12 revolutions of the sails per minute, the millstones will run at 120 r.p.m.

Millstones are usually between 4 feet and 4 feet 8 inches in diameter, each weighing 15 cwt. or so, and are commonly of two types. 'French' stones, made from blocks of hard quartzite from near Paris, backed off with cement or plaster, were used mainly for flour milling as they give a fine flour with large flakes of bran, suitable for 'dressing' into white flour. 'Grey' or 'peak' stones are made from a single block of millstone grit, a hard sandstone from Derbyshire, and were used mainly for grinding general cereals and other items for animal feeds. These do not last as long as French stones, which can run for 100 years or more before wearing out. In earlier times 'Blue' or 'Cullen' stones were used for flour milling; they were made from a single piece of lava quarried in the Cologne area of Germany but none now survive in use. They sometimes remain as paving stones or doorsteps and a good example can be seen at Hibaldstow. The most recent type of stone is the 'composition' stone, made from a type of concrete with emery or crushed French stone chips as aggregate. Sometimes an old grey or French stone would be refaced with composition to extend its working life. Such stones are difficult to recognise in place as they resemble their 'host' stone.

The tentering gear, which regulates the gap between the stones according to their speed of rotation, is usually controlled by a single governor, usually of the centrifugal type but occasionally of the 'lag' type as at Heckington. This is driven either by gears from the foot of the upright shaft or by belt. Most mills use very compact iron bridgetrees to support the stone spindle (on which the upper or 'runner' stone pivots).

Auxiliary machines were once common, such as flour dressers, grain cleaners, corn crushers (or roller mills), kibblers (small cast iron 'millstones' for coarse grinding) and mixers (for making up animal feed from various ingredients). Few remain, most mills only retaining the basic millstones and sack hoist.

Other uses for windpower included grinding chalk for whiting, sawing timber, grinding mustard, producing oil and pumping water. In Lincolnshire only the last of these categories can be found now with the exception of traces of whiting mill machinery in the mill at Market Place, Barton upon Humber, which carried out this function prior to its conversion to a flour mill.

Pumping mills were once common in the south of the county where they were usually smock mills, used to drain the fens by means of scoopwheels, which push water from a low level to a higher one, rather like a water-wheel in reverse. All have gone now due to the introduction of steam, and later diesel and electric pumping stations. Some mills were moved and converted to corn mills, as at Dyke Mill near Bourne. The only remains of a fen mill can be seen at Amber Hill in Holland Fen near Boston where the stump of a tower mill survives with its scoopwheel which was engine driven until the 1950's.

Pumping windmills were also used in large numbers by the brick and tile works around the coast and along the Humber estuary (see illustration p.8). These were much smaller in scale than the fen mills and used lift pumps to de-water the claypits. The earlier ones were miniature windmills, either being small tower mills or skeletal timber mills of uncertain type, being a cross between a post and a smock mill. They used either common or spring sails and drove the pump directly via a cranked 'windshaft' and a connecting rod. A plain wheel on the windshaft acted as brakewheel and they were kept into the wind by means of a large vane. Later examples were of the iron-framed 'annular' type, which were also used for pumping water from wells for houses and farms. Many of these survive but they are beyond the scope of this book. However, the earlier types are now very rare and the only examples known to the author are the derelict tower mill near Sutton on Sea and a dismantled skeleton mill now at Waltham windmill centre, which formerly stood at a brickworks near North Thoresby (grid reference TF319989). Remains of other windpumps can still be seen around disused brickyards, but most have now virtually disappeared, in some cases literally swallowed up by the land they once helped to drain.

Millers and Millwrights

These two specialised trades have existed for centuries and have only declined in the last 100 years or so. A glance at any mid-19th century trades directory will show just how many millers there once were in Lincolnshire, virtually every village having at least one, almost all at windmills or watermills. In many cases a family would operate several mills and sons often followed their fathers into the business. A notable Lincolnshire example was the Hoyle family, with mills at Alford, Maltby le Marsh and Mareham le Fen.

Millwrights were a special blend of various tradesmen, encompassing carpentry, joinery, iron and brass founding, engineering, millstone building and dressing, building and milling. The millwright would usually make the machinery, cap and sails, contracting out the construction of the tower and floors to bricklayers and carpenters, while retaining close control over their work. In the case of post mills, and probably also of smock mills, the millwright would make the whole of the structure as well.

The usual method of erecting a new mill would be for the miller to commission the work but sometimes an entrepreneur would pay for a mill's construction and then lease it out to tenant millers. Millwrights occasionally did this themselves, as probably happened at Waltham. Nineteenth century directories list a number of millwrighting firms and individuals. Several of these subsequently developed into well-known engineering firms, such as Tuxfords of Boston, Marshall of Gainsborough, Ruston and Foster, both of Lincoln. Other firms continued to specialise in traditional millwrighting and several survived into the present century, such as Saunderson and Son of Louth, and Robert Thompson and Son of Alford. Saundersons were well-known for their elegant tower mills, several fine examples surviving in the area. They also built windmills in other counties and had the distinction of building the last new windmill in the country at Much Hadham, Hertfordshire, in 1892-3 (a very large eight-sail mill, now demolished).

Thompsons of Alford are the only firm remaining in business in the county. They can trace their origins back into the 18th century when the Alford millwright was Sam Oxley. He met an unfortunate although not inappropriate end by falling from the top of a windmill at Barrow in 1829, aged 70. By this time however the firm was being run by Richard Oxley and he was followed in turn by John Oxley. By 1855 he had died and his widow Ann was running the firm, although the work was actually supervised by Edward Wheatcroft who had been at the firm since his youth in the 1830's. By 1868 he was in sole charge but in 1881, 26 year old Robert Thompson, from Hull, was in control of the firm. He remained, with his son Jack latterly, well into the present century. Jack Thompson died in the 1970's, but the business continued under Jim Davies. He is now semi-retired, with his son Tom carrying on the work. Several people are employed, with continuity being assured by the practice of training youngsters as apprentices. They work all over the country, mostly on windmills. Much of their work is now concerned with the complete restoration of mills or repairs to preserved examples but they still maintain several working mills, carrying out whatever day to day repairs are necessary. Such is the demand for their work that the order books are full for several years ahead and they are assured of a long and prosperous future in their ancient workshops in Parsons Lane, off West Street.

Preservation and the Future

Lincolnshire's windmills have been decimated since the war to the point where so few retain caps or even machinery that those which do really ought to be given some protection if at all possible. Sibsey mill should be safe enough in the hands of the Department of the Environment, as should the mills cared for by Lincolnshire County Council at Alford, Burgh le Marsh and Heckington and by Cleethorpes District Council at Waltham. Other mills are looked after by their owners or local groups, such as those at Lincoln, Kirton Lindsey and Wrawby.

One mill whose future is less certain at present is the fine Maud Foster mill at Boston. This was restored in the early 1950's but is now in need of major attention, having received little or no maintenance since then. As it stands in commercial premises it is unlikely to receive much help unless central or local government aid can be secured. Other mills stand fairly complete, but without caps and a few are completely derelict. Those most deserving of preservation are the giant Moulton mill, the midget Sutton on Sea windpump and the elderly Lutton mill.

The remainder are mainly left to their own devices; occasionally an owner will conserve or even partly restore a tower, the mills at Sturton by Stow, Maltby le Marsh and Grainthorpe being examples of this. The house-conversion of mills is a controversial subject to mill enthusiasts. As stated above, so few windmills remain with their machinery intact that any attempt to house-convert such mills should be strongly resisted and some other way of restoring or conserving the mills sought. The trouble with house conversion is that machinery invariably gets in the way so is usually removed, in the process destroying any technological value the mill may have had. Windmills are primarily *machines* for grinding corn, not buildings which happen to have machinery in them. On the other hand, an already gutted mill can actually benefit from some form of conversion (usually residential) where this can actually preserve what is an otherwise largely useless structure. An example of this can be seen at Scunthorpe where what little remains of the machinery has been retained and the exterior has been restored by the erection of a replica cap. The dividing line can be very difficult to establish.

The most encouraging aspect of mill preservation is the way in which individuals or organisations have taken on the restoration of what would formerly have been 'write-offs'. The best known in the recent past have been the complete rebuild of Ellis's mill, Lincoln, by Lincoln Civic Trust, preceded by the equally complete reconstruction of Wrawby post mill in the mid 1960's, one of the first such projects to be undertaken in this country, and since emulated in other areas such as East Anglia. Currently work is being carried out, or is planned, on mills at Swineshead, Horncastle and Lutton.

An allied topic to preservation and conversion is the 'cannibalisation' of parts from disused mills to make up the gaps in a restoration project. Generally speaking, I feel that this is a bad practice and should be discouraged. It is easy for a mill restorer to justify the removal of redundant machinery, or fittings, to the owner of a disused, but complete mill tower for example, on the grounds that the items 'will be put to good use'. However, once the machinery is taken out it becomes just another gutted tower, ripe for house conversion or even demolition. Had it retained its gear for a few years longer, a new owner might have embarked upon restoration himself, resulting in two restored mills instead of one. There are exceptions to this philosophy of course; in the case of a mill which is to be demolished or converted anyway, or where so little remains as to make any reconstruction unlikely, it is better that any usable gear is salvaged, even if no particular 'home' for it has been found in a mill. In this way machinery has been salvaged in recent years from house converted mills at Belton and Epworth, and from a demolished mill at Saxby All Saints. If machinery is missing from a mill under repair, in my opinion it is better to make new items; 'wrought iron' components can be fabricated from mild steel, iron castings are readily available and surprisingly economical, and timber wheels etc. can easily be made in the traditional manner. Making new components in this way helps to keep old skills alive in our increasingly electronic age and is a far more honest way to restore a mill than to rob others and try to integrate bits and pieces from various sources.

About this Survey, and Acknowledgements

I have been searching out windmills since 1969 and looked at some of the Lincolnshire mills before 1974, including several lesser-known remains. The main survey was carried out in 1977 and 1978 however, with follow-up visits in 1982, 1983 and 1985. I have stayed loyal to the 'old' county of Lincolnshire, comprising the parts of Lindsey, Kesteven and Holland, partly for historical reasons and partly out of nostalgia. All the more complete mills have been revisited in 1985 and many others checked in passing although I cannot guarantee to have up to date information on every site. The interiors of as many mills as possible have been inspected, to see what machinery or other items of interest may remain. I hope I have visited every site where something substantial remains; in addition a great many other sites have been checked, mostly with nothing remaining except perhaps an odd millstone or two as garden ornaments or a ring of foundations at ground level. Each mill has been photographed and where interior machinery is present details have been taken of this. A preliminary report was prepared and circulated to interested parties in 1979, with many useful leads being forthcoming as a result.

My main sources of information have been the 1824 and 1962 one-inch ordnance survey maps and the 1905-8 six-inch ordnance survey map, Rex Wailes' Newcomen Society papers (see the bibliography for details), the Simmons collection and other material held by the Lincolnshire Mill Archive, the Exley collection, census returns and trades directories held by Lincoln Reference Library and manuscript maps and other material held by the Lincolnshire Record Office.

Particular thanks go to Les Osborne, the secretary of Lincolnshire Mills Group for his assistance with research; Jon Sass, the Chairman of Lincolnshire Mills Group for his detailed help with mills in the North of the county; Chris Wilson for his valuable knowledge of mills throughout the county since the late 1940's; the staff of Lincolnshire Record Office, Lincoln Reference Library and the Museum of Lincolnshire Life, and to Mrs. Catherine Wilson of Lincolnshire County Council's Recreational Services Department for her enthusiasm for this book and help in getting it published. Help from David Pearce, Mr. R. Hawksley, John Mullett, Roy Gregory, Adrian Lewis, Nigel Moon, Mark Barnard, Arthur Smith and Ron Pocklington is also gratefully acknowledged.

I must also thank the owners of the various mills listed in this book, and the owners of the vanished mill sites who almost without exception have been friendly and helpful in allowing me access to examine or to photograph their mills. In closing, I must point out to anyone seeking to follow in my footsteps, that every mill or site has an owner, whose permission should be sought before any examination is attempted.

Photographs are by the author unless noted otherwise.

Heybridge, Essex
December 1985

HORNCASTLE

Cross from Spital Hill, Gainsborough

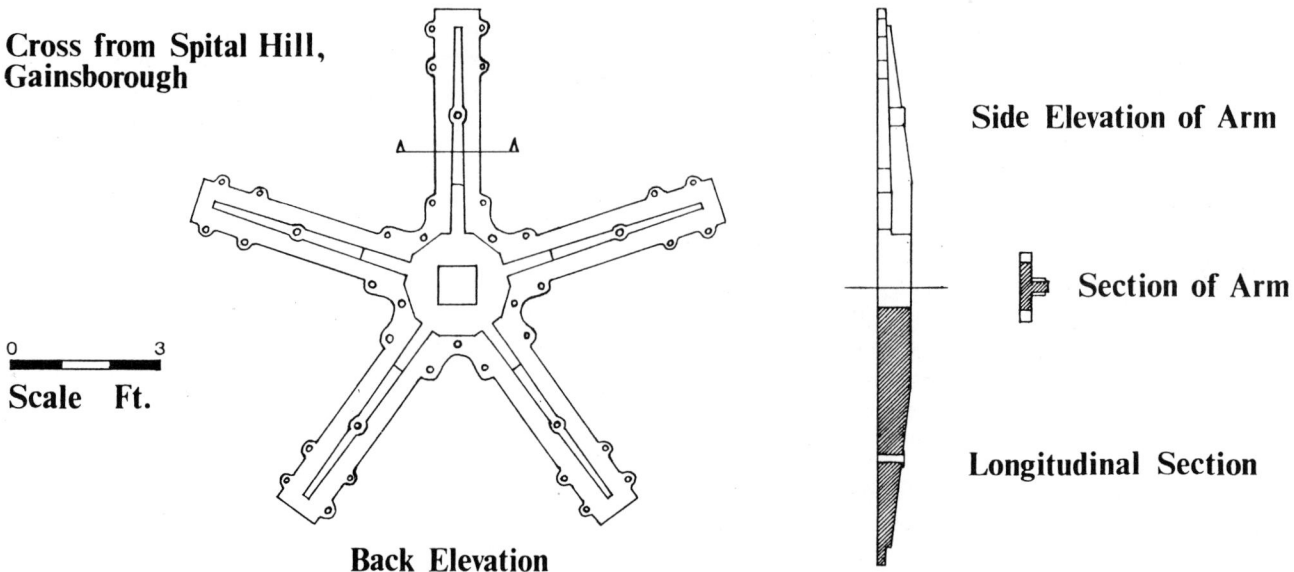

Scale Ft. 0–3

Back Elevation

Side Elevation of Arm

Section of Arm

Longitudinal Section

Based on a drawing by David Pearce

SUTTON ON SEA

Brickworks Pumping Mill

Conjectural Reconstruction

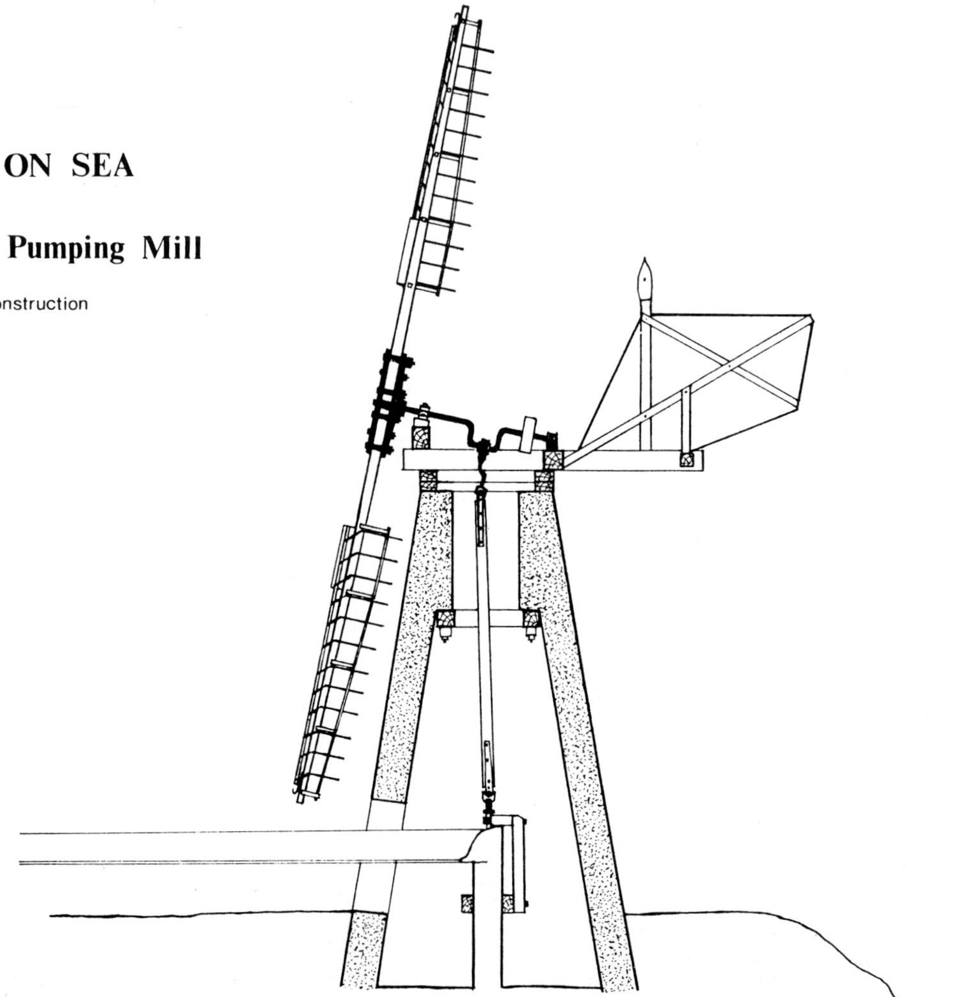

Scale Ft. 0–5

Peter Dolman 1985

MOULTON MILL

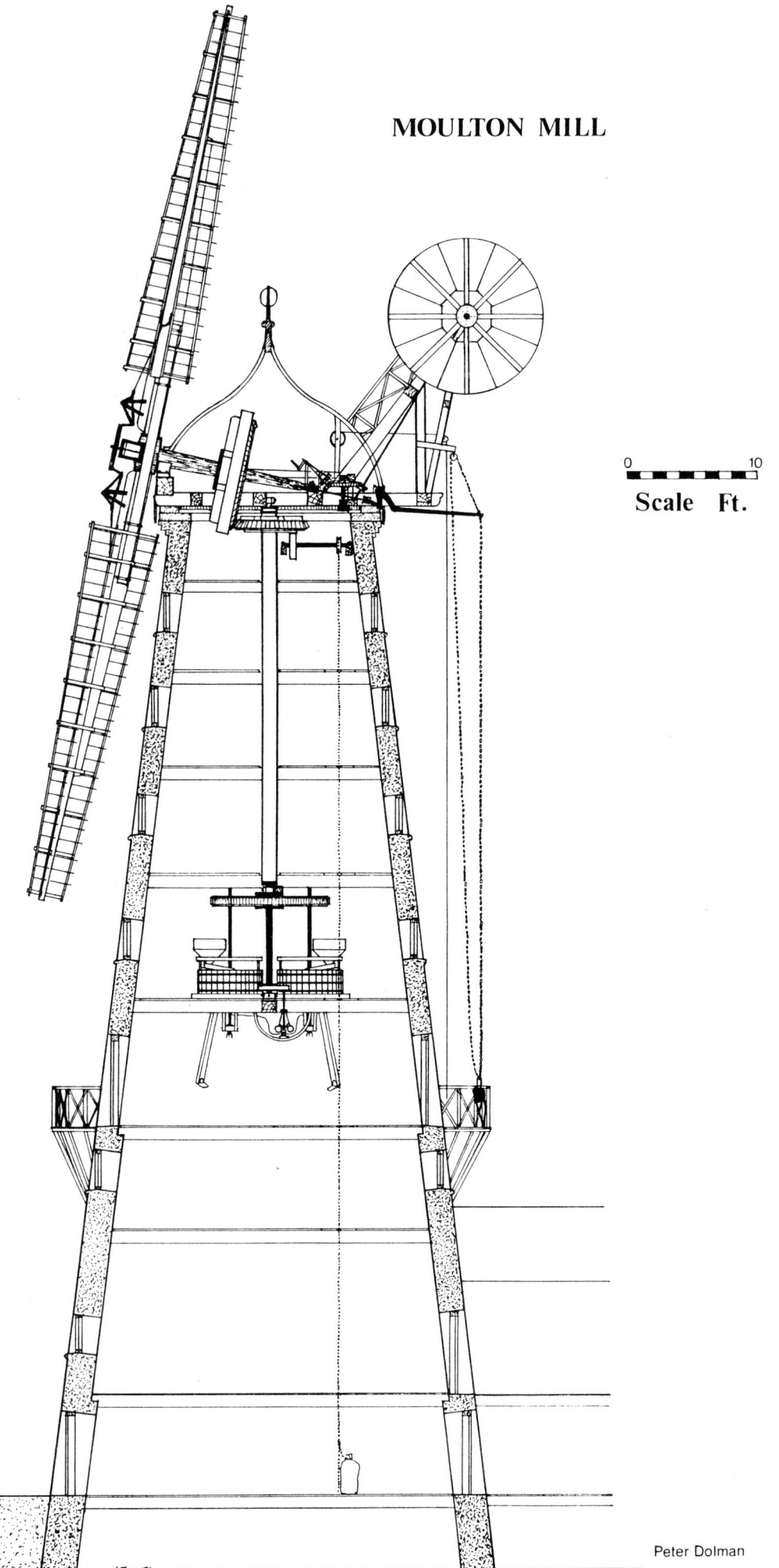

Scale Ft. 0 — 10

Peter Dolman 1985

LINCOLNSHIRE WINDMILLS — GAZETTEER

Date of visit is indicated by the year and whether the interior or merely the exterior was inspected. 6-figure Ordnance Survey grid references are given, including the preceding letters. Mills marked (H) now stand in the county of Humberside.

1. Addlethorpe TF552675 'Ingoldmells Mill' 1973, 1974, 1983, 1984 int.

Built to replace a post mill c.1830, this tall tower mill worked by wind until 1944. The four patent sails drove three pairs of stones on the third floor, originally two French and one grey, but latterly two grey and one French. The French stones were taken out c.1920 and replaced with a kibbler as no flour has been made since the Great War. The sails were removed in 1949 and the cap followed suit in 1968. Milling continued by Blackstone oil engine power using the stones, with a new diesel engine being installed in 1960, itself replaced in 1962 following problems. It went out of use shortly afterwards however as electric motors took over any grinding or cleaning work with modern machinery, still in use today.

The tarred tower stands derelict, has lost its stage and has a very pronounced lean. The lower part of the upright shaft remains with the great spur wheel and all the gearing and fittings to the two pairs of grey stones, with the kibbler, engine and drive shafts. The owner wishes to reduce the tower to a stump due to concern over its stability. When this happens the machinery will be removed and taken into safe storage by mill enthusiasts for future use or display elsewhere. The engine is to be taken to Burgh le Marsh mill for preservation.

2. Alford TF457765 Hoyle's Mill 1973, 1974, 1978, 1985 int.

This well-proportioned tower mill was built by Oxley, the local millwright, in 1813, reputedly on the site of an earlier post mill. If this is the case then the post mill had a short life for it is not shown on a map of 1790. It worked until 1955 and in 1957 was acquired by Banks Bros. of Kirton in Lindsey who repaired it and set it to work again. It is still worked occasionally by the miller, Mr. C. F. W. Banks and is now owned by Lincolnshire County Council, who maintain it in first-class condition, aided by the fact that the country's last traditional millwrighting firm, R. Thompson and Sons are based in the town and can keep a close eye on the mill. The present head of the firm, Jim Davies, states that in his opinion the mill is 'the best in England', this being not merely local pride, but based on his wide experience of repairing mills the length and breadth of the country, and one which the author does not dispute.

The mill is powered by five single sided patent sails, which were renewed together with the cap in 1978 by Thompsons. The tarred tower has a stage at second floor level and a raised loading stage at ground floor level, a common feature of Lincolnshire mills. The ground floor contains a hurst frame with a pair of grey stones, formerly driven by engine by way of a pair of fast and loose pulleys outside. The first floor is empty and was used for storage. One of the second floor supports is made from the end of a post mill crosstree and still has the double birdsmouth and mortice in it where the quarter bar (or 'spurn') once fitted. The second floor is the spout floor, with the iron bridge trees and single governor. The third floor contains the stones. Originally there were three pairs, two French and one grey, but at some stage a further pair of greys has been added. The mill is very powerful and has been known to drive all four pairs together in a strong breeze. The drive to the stones is by the usual arrangement of an iron great spur wheel with mortice stone nuts on quants. The fourth floor is the bin floor and also contains a reel-type smutter, driven off a small inverted crown wheel on the upright shaft. The fifth floor is empty and the sixth is the dust floor immediately under the cap. The wallower is of iron with the sackhoist, which uses an endless chain, driven directly from the underside by friction. The brake wheel is wooden with clasp arms and bolted-on iron teeth and an iron brake.

The mill forms an attractive group with the adjacent house and bakery. It is intended to restore the other buildings shortly and to open up the mill more frequently to the public, access being limited to open days at present.

3. Alford TF444755 Wallace's or Station Mill 1974, 1978

One of the oldest tower mills in the area, this was standing by 1790 and worked until about 1930, being dismantled in 1933. The cap and windshaft were still in place in 1950 but later in the 1950's it was partly demolished. There were four patent sails driving three pairs of stones, two grey and one French. The two storeyed stump stands beside the mill house.

4. Alkborough (H) SE883215 1978, 1983 int.

Until at least 1853 a post mill stood here but at some time after this a tower mill was built on top of the original roundhouse wall. The mill ceased work by wind in 1916 but continued to work by engine for a little while.

The tower stands roofless and derelict with the remains of all the floors in place. Of the machinery, only two of the three pairs of stones remain, one of French, the other having a French bedstone and a grey runner. Now that the tar has worn off the tower and most of the internal plaster has fallen off it is possible to see the join between roundhouse and tower clearly. The original piers have been cut back flush with the wall, except under the floor, which they help to support. The holes for the projecting crosstrees and quarter bars have been crudely filled in with brickwork. The floors contain re-used timber from the post mill and two posts are made from a common sail whip.

5. Amber Hill TF229460 Holland Fen 1978 int.

This tower mill was one of several pumping windmills once standing in Holland Fen and probably dates from the late 18th or early 19th century. Late in the 19th century it was converted to steam power and continued to work, driven by traction engine and finally by tractor until about 1960. The scoopwheel was rebuilt in 1960 by the owner, Mr. Clark and a joiner from Heckington, Gerald Woods. It now stands as a roofed stump at about half its former height with the scoopwheel adjacent and is kept in good order.

6. Barnetby le Wold (H) TA066096 1978, 1985

This small tower mill probably dates from the early 19th century and worked by wind until the spring of 1904 when the sails were blown off. It worked by engine until the 1930's and was then left to become derelict. It now stands as a roofless tower with all of the floors collapsed. The last remaining stones, a pair with a French bedstone and a grey runner, together with another grey bedstone, were taken out in 1964. The lower section of the iron upright shaft remains with the iron great spur wheel and another wheel connected with the engine drive.

7. Barrow upon Humber (H) TA 062229 Barrow Haven 1978, 1985

Built in 1816, this tower mill had patent sails and three pairs of stones, two French and one grey. It had gone out of use by the Great War and is now an empty shell.

8. Barrow upon Humber (H) TA059216 Pearson's Mill 1978, 1985

This tower mill was built in 1869 and worked until about 1920, when it was partly demolished. It had four patent sails. The shortened tower, with a crenelated top, is used as a garage and store.

9. Barton upon Humber (H) TA027226 Hewson's Mill 1978, 1983, 1985

This large eight storeyed tower mill was one of three mills on Barton Waterside, the other two probably both being used as whiting mills. Hewson's mill was built in 1813 when Messrs. Cook and Sutton were the owners. It was fitted with 'Sutton's Patent Gravitated Sails for Windmills'; these had longitudinal shutters each side of the back which could be 'feathered' and were controlled by chain and weights, like 'Cubitt's patent' sails. They were patented in 1807 by William Hesledon but never became as popular as the more successful Cubitt design. Being a large mill it was costly to erect and as a result Cook and Sutton became bankrupt in 1816. It was put up for sale, being described as 60 feet high to the top of the tower, 12 feet diameter at the top and 26 feet diameter at the bottom (presumably internally). There were three pairs of French stones, one pair of grey stones, '2 large cylinders' (flour dressers), and a corn screen, or cleaner. It was put up for sale several times in its early days and 1848 was described as having a steam mill contiguous to the tower 'well adapted for the purpose of corn millers and seed or bone crushers'. Whether these other trades were ever carried out is unlikely for from the late 1840's it entered a settled phase with the Hewson family who ran it until it ceased work. It was working by wind up to the Great War but by 1922 was reduced to engine power; it appears to have ceased work in the late 1920's. There were four double sided patent sails controlled from a stage at third floor level. The tower stands derelict with no cap or windows but the cap frame is still in place. The machinery is presumed to have been entirely removed.

10. Barton upon Humber (H) TA032217 Market Place 1978, 1983 int., 1985

This imposing, tall tower mill has a very unusual history and has been the subject of controversy more than once in its long career. It appears to have been erected or perhaps just raised in 1810 to replace another tower mill by Thomas Marris. It is shown in an engraving of 1810 quite prominently, although in the distance, possibly because of its newness. It had six sails and was used as a whiting mill (grinding chalk into a fine powder for use in various industries such as starch, putty and paint making). Following Marris' death in 1815 it was advertised again with three pairs of stones (two pairs of 'Blue' stones and one of grey stones) 'lately fitted up'. Also 'part of the building. . . may be converted into a malt-kiln or starch manufactory' and there was a 'Barley mill attached for the purpose of making French and Pearl Barley'.

The sails were apparently taken down in 1868 on the orders of the Town Council after one fell off into the adjoining road. It was then driven by a large gas engine, fed from the town gasworks. At one time it was worked by members of the Hewson family who had the tower mill mentioned above but it ended its working life about 1950 under Day's.

It stands without its cap, but retaining much of the machinery and the iron curb. The upper section of the upright shaft is missing, but the large square wooden lower section remains. The great spur wheel is of a rather elegant timber clasp-arm construction with paired spokes and an iron tooth-ring. The stone nuts and quants are missing but the three pairs of stones remain on the third floor. Two pairs are French, the third having a grey bedstone and a French runner, which has been refaced on its back and carries the date 1919. On the spout floor the lower stone spindles remain but only one iron bridgetree is left. Just above first floor level is an iron spur wheel of about 18 inches diameter which would have driven the edge runners of the original whiting mill on the ground floor through a second upright shaft (as can still be seen at Hessle whiting mill on the opposite bank of the Humber). The upright shaft ends just under the first floor with a short iron section where formerly two iron bevel wheels engaged with one on the upright shaft, one carrying the drive into the adjoining shed, where the 'Barley Mill' was once situated, the other taking the drive from the engine, the concrete base of which can be seen.

The mill is at present disused but in fairly good condition and in 1985 was the subject of a public enquiry over its proposed demolition to make way for a supermarket. It is now hoped to preserve the tower with its gear and to convert the attached buildings, the threat of demolition having been lifted following the enquiry.

11. Baston TF116132 Hudson's Mill 1971, 1974, 1983 int.

Said to have been built in 1806, this tower mill worked until the Great War and was then dismantled. The machinery is thought to have been taken to another mill. It had four patent sails and probably drove two pairs of stones. The stone tower, once rendered, stands on a low mound (which suggests an older mill site) and is now virtually a shell with only a few floor beams remaining. Part of the cap frame lingers on at the top. In its later working life it lost a sail when a wagon came too close for comfort.

12. Belton (H) SE770075 Westgate 1978, 1982 int., 1985

Erected in the early 19th century, this tower mill worked by wind, latterly with only two sails, until the early 1930's, after which it was engine driven until 1960. It had patent sails and drove three pairs of stones, two of French and one of greys. By 1978 only one pair of stones remained, with the lower part of the upright shaft, steelyards, governor and one bridgetree. This gear was taken in 1980 and stored at North Leverton mill in Nottinghamshire. The iron bridgetree has since found its way to Bardwell in Suffolk, where the tower mill has been put back to work. Belton mill was converted into a house between 1982 and 1984 and now sports a dummy cap together with a huge modern house on the side which rather spoils the otherwise well-intentioned attempt to restore its appearance.

13. Billinghay TF153551 1974, 1977

Like several other mills in the county the builders of this tower mill in 1844 decided to utilize the earlier walls of a post mill roundhouse. It had four patent sails and worked until early 1938 by wind, losing its sails in 1939. There were two pairs of French stones and one of greys, plus a further two pairs which were engine driven. The upper part of the tower was removed in the 1960's and only the derelict two storeyed stump remains.

14. Billinghay TF143551 1977

This tower mill was described as being 'newly erected' in 1806. Later in the century it was raised from 5 to 7 storeys in height. It worked until early 1945 when the four remaining sails were taken down. There were six patent sails, driving two pairs of grey and one pair of French stones. It was also reduced in height during the 1960's and the two storeyed stump is a store.

15. Bilsby TF470766 1973, 1974, 1978 int., 1985 int.

This tower mill is said to have replaced a post mill in 1861; however I consider that it could be older than this, possibly of early 19th century date. It has been raised from 4 to 5 storeys in height and was once hand-winded by wheel and endless chain. It worked by wind until 1932, carrying on for a number of years after with an engine. There were four patent sails driving three pairs of stones, of which two pairs of greys remain. One pair has iron spur gearing underneath for engine drive. Access to the mill is difficult due to an accumulation of rubbish but most of the gear is believed to remain. The tower stands capless and derelict.

16. Blyton SK852948 1978 int.

Built in 1825 this tower mill worked until 1910 by wind. It carried on by engine, followed by electricity, until the late 1960's. A new observatory-type top was put on in 1974 and the tower is now preserved. There were four patent sails, driving three pairs of stones. Of the original gear, only the curb and one grey bedstone remains. Later gear consisting of a roller mill and a hurst frame with a pair of grey stones also survives.

17. Bolingbroke TF339642 Old Bolingbroke 1977

This tower mill was probably built in the early 19th century but could possibly be late eighteenth century. It was unusually short with only three storeys and worked until 1950 when one arm broke off the cross. It was dismantled in 1953, two of the sails being taken to Heckington mill. There were four patent sails driving one pair of French and one pair of grey stones. The tower was converted into a clubhouse in the 1970's when it gained an additional storey, giving it an appearance similar to that at Bilsby.

18. Boston TF332447 Maud Foster or Ostler's Mill, Skirbeck 1971, 1974, 1982 int.

One of the best sited and proportioned mills in Lincolnshire, this beautiful tower mill was erected for Thomas and Isaac Reckitt in 1819 by the Hull millwrights Norman and Smithson. The original drawings and accounts survive, telling us that it cost £1826-10s-6d, which was a large sum in those days. It shows just how far advanced millwrighting was in this area by 1819, with all iron gearing, patent sails and a tall, well proportioned tower. It worked until 1942 and was preserved as a landmark in 1953, the last of more than a dozen mills in the town.

There are five patent sails, the shutters of which are now at Wrawby mill. An unusual feature is the weather beam (or 'rode balk') which is of cast iron, probably a replacement of the original wooden one. The brake wheel is of wooden clasp-arm type with an iron tooth ring and wooden brake. The wallower is also of iron with a wooden friction drive to the sackhoist. The dust floor is more spacious than is often found in Lincolnshire and is lit by windows, a welcome change from the gloomy, cramped space usually encountered by mill explorers! Three pairs of stones, two grey and one French, survive on the fourth floor with vats, spouts etc. all intact. The great spur wheel is of iron, as is the upright shaft. The stone nuts have wooden cogs, as usual. The spout floor gives access to the reefing stage and contains a fine governor which controls all three pairs of stones. The bridge trees are of iron and are Y shaped, with integral bridging boxes. The lower floors have been utilized for various purposes since the mill ceased work and are in rather poor condition. The mill itself is in reasonable condition, although the cap and sails are beginning to show their age. Unfortunately the mill stands in the midst of business premises and so is not open for public viewing. The owners are unable to maintain it themselves and at the time of writing the mill's long term future is yet to be decided. It is hoped to secure its preservation eventually though, for this is the second-best known building in Boston, after the 'Stump'.

19. Bourne TF 096212 1971, 1983

This mill was rebuilt in 1832 when the old stone tower was raised to six storeys in height. It worked until 1915 when it was dismantled following lightning damage. It had four patent sails and drove three pairs of stones. The two storeyed stump remains, used as a store.

20. Bourne TF103226 Dyke Mill 1971, 1974, 1983

The only smock mill to remain in Lincolnshire, this was originally a pumping mill in Deeping Fen, probably dating fom the 18th century. In about 1845 it was moved to Dyke and fitted with corn milling machinery. It ceased work in the mid 1920's and was dismantled in 1926. It had a boat-shaped cap turned to wind by a braced tailpole, both features inherited from its former use. It had two common and two spring shuttered sails, driving three pairs of stones. The empty tower is now used as a store.

21. Brigg (H) SE 996065 Bell's Mill 1978 int.

Built in 1836-7 by the local millwrights James Hart and Son for the sum of £900, this tower mill worked by wind until c.1920/1 when one of the sails was lost. It continued to be power driven until c.1956 when it was gutted and modernised. The tower stands disused, the only machinery remaining being the upper wooden section of the upright shaft and the iron wallower. There were four double sided patent sails.

22. Broughton (H) SE 986072 Castlethorpe Mill 1978, 1983 int.

This stoutly built tower mill was erected in 1804 and worked by wind until 1911 when it was gutted by fire. It was rebuilt and refitted in 1924 as a steam mill with new floors and an iron-framed hurst with two pairs of stones on the ground floor. These were latterly driven by oil engine and it ceased work finally in about 1960. The machinery was removed in 1982 and when inspected in 1983 it was empty and disused. It has since been converted into a restaurant.

23. Burgh le Marsh TF503649 Dobson's Mill 1974 int., 1977, 1985 int.

One of the best preserved of the County's mills, this tower mill was built in 1813 by Oxley of Alford. It is shown on an Estate map of 1819 as having four sails. These are said to have been common sails operated from a stage but in my opinion it has always had patent sails. The stage is now missing but the filled-in putlog holes can be made out at second floor level, where the two door openings have been partly filled in and converted to windows. As the stage only relied on the putlogs for support it cannot have been wide enough to reef common sails from. I also believe it could have originally had five sails as it does at present, like Alford mill which was also erected in 1813 by Oxley. Unlike Alford mill however this mill has 'left-handed' sails, that is they rotate clockwise when viewed from the front. It worked by wind, assisted by an oil engine latterly, until 1964 when Edwin Dobson gave up the business. The following year it was acquired by Lindsey County Council who wished to preserve it for future generations. In 1974 Lincolnshire County Council took over and in 1984 it was set to work again, staffed by volunteer millers on special open days. It is open to the public during the day and there is an adjacent shop where souvenirs may be bought.

The five patent sails drive through a composite brake wheel with iron hub, spokes and teeth and a wooden rim. The brake band is also of iron. The wallower is of iron with mortised wooden cogs, an unusual type in the County. The sackhoist is driven from the underside of the wallower and as is often found uses an endless chain which saves having to lower the chain after each sack is raised.

There are two bin floors, both divided up by partitions and the stones are on the second floor. The two pairs of greys and one pair of French are driven in the usual manner by an iron great spur wheel, mortice stone nuts and an iron upright shaft. A fourth 'nut' engages with the spur wheel and formerly took the drive from the auxiliary oil engine. By putting the wallower out of gear it was possible to then drive the 'wind' stones by engine if desired.

The first floor, in addition to containing the windmill tentering gear, governor and spouts, has a pair of grey stones directly underdriven from the engine by way of bevel gears. The ground floor contains more engine-driven machinery consisting of a Hunt Corn Crushing Mill (or roller mill), a mixer by Thompsons of Alford (for making up animal feeds) and an elevator for moving stock around when the wind-powered hoist is not in use. The Blackstone diesel engine from Addlethorpe mill is to be installed to replace the original which had been disposed of.

24. Burgh le Marsh TF497650 Hanson's Mill 1974, 1977, 1985

There was a post mill on this site until at least 1842 but in 1855 a 'newly erected' tower mill was advertised for sale. It worked until the 1930's and lost its sails in 1938. In 1964 the upright shaft, spur gearing, one pair of stones and other items were taken to Brixton mill in London where they were used in the restoration by Thompsons of Alford. There were four patent sails, driving two pairs of French and one pair of grey stones. At the time of writing the tower stands derelict with the cap frame in position and some machinery in the tower, including a flour dresser. Regretably in 1985 permission to demolish the mill was granted and it is likely to be replaced by housing. In view of its excellent site in the middle of the village it seems to me to be a wasted opportunity to preserve an interesting structure, which could easily have been converted to residential use. It is hoped to salvage the surviving machinery when demolition takes place.

25. Burton upon Stather (H) SE874172 1978 int.

This post mill, similar in appearance to Wrawby mill, had the date 1732 on its brakewheel, which may have indicated when it was built. It probably gained its roundhouse in the late 18th or early 19th century and worked until early this century after which it became derelict. It was demolished in the late 1920's and all that remains now is the tapering brick shell of the roundhouse.

26. Butterwick TF385455 1977 int.

Built in 1871, this tower mill worked by wind until the mid 1920's. It carried on using an engine for many years after this. It now stands disused and is rapidly decaying as the tower is no longer roofed over. It had four patent sails which drove two, and possibly three pairs of stones. At any rate, three pairs of stones remain, two of greys and one of French. One of the pairs of greys is fitted up with a direct underdrive by engine through a pair of bevel wheels and fast and loose pulleys outside the tower. Its runner is fitted with a 'damsel', a very unusual feature in a county where overdrive is virtually universal. The gearing is all iron, with mortice stone nuts. The upright shaft's upper section and the old sackhoist are missing, since direct engine drive was employed latterly and a rather neat 'slack chain' sackhoist has been arranged from the horizontal engine drive shaft.

27. Caistor TA125007 Wright's Mill 1978

This small tower mill was probably erected in the early 19th century; it went out of use in 1908 after the cap and sails were blown off in a tail-wind. There were four patent sails, driving three pairs of stones. The empty tower stands as a store.

28. Carrington TF294573 Watkinson's Mill, New Bolingbroke 1973

Described as being 'newly erected' in 1821, this tower mill worked until 1944 when the weather beam broke, continuing by engine for a while after this. It was originally driven by two roller reefing sails and two common sails but ended its life with four patent sails. There were two pairs of stones, one grey and one French. The upper two storeys have been removed and the stump is used as a store.

29. Carrington TF307585 Rundle's Mill, New Bolingbroke 1973

This tower mill probably dates from the early or mid 19th century and has been disused since 1906 at least. Little is known of its original equipment, only one pair of stones remaining in 1985, when they were removed. The iron spur wheel and upright shaft survived until the early 1980's when they were taken out. The tower is in good condition, although some floors are bad, and is used for storage in connection with the adjacent foundry.

30. Corringham SK879909 1978

This little tower mill probably dates from the early 19th century and had gone out of use by 1908. It has been a shell for many years and no machinery remains, apart from the iron curb.

31. Corringham SK863916 Winter's Mill 1978 int.

Like the other mill in the village, little is known about this tower mill. It is probably also an early 19th century mill and had also ceased to work by 1908. Unlike the other mill however some vestiges of the floors and gear, in the form of a pair of stones, remain. There is also a water tank in the tower, and the mill has been used as a water tower for many years.

32. Cowbit TF265179 1972, 1983

Erected in 1798 as a short, well 'battered' mill, this tower mill was later raised by another floor, resulting in a rather pleasing concave tower which survives today. This work may have been carried out shortly before 1815, when it is described as being 'newly built', although such statements should be carefully vetted as auctioneers can be rather over generous in their descriptions of property, then as now! It worked by wind until the mid 1930's and then continued by engine, and finally by electric motor until 1969 when it closed down, subsequently being gutted of all machinery. The original gear had been taken out many years previously. Four patent sails drove three pairs of stones, two grey and one French. The tower is in good condition and is used for storage.

33. Croft TF501596 1977, 1985

This tower mill was built in 1814 as a four storeyed mill. In 1859 it was raised by an incredible three storeys, the new portion being built up vertically to use the old cap. The resulting mill looked rather odd and the whole scheme was probably made necessary by the erection of a tall granary by the mill which would otherwise have robbed it of wind. In this form it worked until the late 1940's, latterly on two sails after a tailwinding in 1944. The cap and top two storeys were taken off by late 1949, work being done by an electric hammer mill from then onwards. Up to the time it was taken down, it relied solely on wind power, in the form of four single sided patent sails. The brakewheel was of wooden clasp-arm construction with an iron tooth ring. The wallower and the other machinery was of iron, but here the stone nuts were solid and the great spur wheel had morticed wooden cogs, unusual in Lincolnshire. Originally two pairs of French and one of greys were driven, but like most mills it ended up with two pairs of greys and one of French stones following the demise of the flour trade early this century.

34. Crowland TF236101 1971

Probably dating from the late 18th century this small tower mill is thought to have ceased work about 1900. Postcards of the Edwardian era show it to be a three storeyed tower, already without its cap. No details of its equipment have come to light so far and it has been used as a house for many years. The two storeyed stump remains, with a house built onto one side.

35. Donington TF218349 Baxter's Mill 1977

This tower mill was standing by 1819 and possibly dates from the 18th century. The sails were removed in 1913 and the mill was then dismantled. It had two common and two spring shuttered sails, which drove two pairs of stones. The tower has been shortened to three storeys in height and has a conical roof. It is used as a store.

36. East Kirkby TF333623 1973, 1978 int., 1985

Said to have been the best mill tower in the county, construction began for William Thimbleby in 1820 by the millwright Sam Ward. Unfortunately he became bankrupt during the course of the work and it was finished by Oxley of Alford, to his usual high standard. It worked by wind until 1927 when the sails were taken off; a pity, as three were almost new. It drove two pairs of French and two pairs of grey stones, originally with four patent sails, but after 1837 with five. After the removal of the sails work continued into the 1950's with an engine-driven hurst on the ground floor. The mill is now a ruin, open to the sky and with all the ironwork removed. Two pairs of stones remain, together with the wooden upper section of the upright shaft.

37. Epworth (H) SE777047 Maw's Mill 1978, 1985 int.

This was one of a group of three tower mills to the north of the village, the others being Brook's mill (described below) and the 'Subscription Mill'. This latter mill had a tablet on it inscribed "This mill is the equal property of subscribers 1805. Both rich and poor a friend will find, who standeth here their corn to grind." It was pulled down in 1921. Maw's mill was built c.1820 and went out of use c.1915. It stood a long way off the road and when the track up to it was impassable by wagons the grain had to be carried by pack horses, which helped to cause its early abandonment. It stood, increasingly derelict, until 1962, when following the fall of one sail the others were removed, together with the cap frame. It now stands in a field, completely derelict and disused. It had four patent sails. Much of the machinery survives in the tower, despite the efforts of vandals to set fire to it. The wallower is of iron, with an integral ring underneath to drive the sackhoist which does not survive. The upright shaft is wood, in two sections, and drove the stones on the second floor. The great spur wheel is of timber clasp-arm construction, with an iron tooth ring. Unfortunately it has broken up and fallen onto the stone floor. Two pairs of French stones and a grey bedstone remain, with all three lower spindles and one set of tentering gear comprising a wooden bridgetree and brayer with an iron steelyard.

On the ground floor were two fireplaces, with the flues passing through the wall to emerge outside at second floor level.

38. Epworth (H) SE781045 Brook's Mill 1978 int., 1982, 1985

This tower mill was built c.1800 and was originally known as the 'White Mill' although like most of its colleagues it ended its working life tarred black, including the cap. It worked by wind until the late 1940's, latterly with two sails, continuing by engine until 1960. The cap and sails were removed in 1962 and the tower was allowed to become derelict. The machinery was removed in 1977, originally intended for use in the restoration of Scunthorpe mill. When this project was abandoned however it was taken into storage and is now at Skidby mill near Hull. The tower, which was an empty shell in 1978, was house-converted in 1982 and has gained a copper-clad mock ogee cap and a large modern house on one side which rather spoils the mill's appearance. It has reverted to its original colour scheme and is now the 'white mill' once again. It had four patent sails which drove three pairs of stones, of which two pairs remained up to 1977, one French and one grey. A further pair of grey stones were engine-driven on a ground floor hurst. A fourth nut engaged the spur wheel, either to take an engine drive or to power auxiliary machinery. The upright shaft was of both wood and iron and the gearing was mostly of iron. Like Maw's mill there were two fireplaces on the ground floor with flues opening out at about first floor level. These had been used this century but were apparently more trouble than they were worth in use. The machinery at Skidby comprises a cast iron great spur wheel 6 feet 2 inches in diameter with 89 teeth, the lower iron upright shaft, with a governor drive gear immediately above its foot, two quants, two mortice stone nuts, one with 20 and one with 18 cogs, three bridge trees, two wood and one iron, a pair of French stones and other miscellaneous items.

30. Epworth (H) SE784034 Thompson's Mill 1978, 1982

Built in the early 19th century this tower mill worked by wind until the 1940's, the two remaining sails only driving the sackhoist in later years, milling being carried out by engine power. The sails had gone by late 1949 and the cap followed suit shortly after. It is said to have continued in occasional use into the 1980's, a hammer mill in the base being driven by tractor. The tower is now becoming rather tatty but still retains most of its machinery. The four patent sails drove three pairs of stones, two French and one grey.

40. Faldingworth TF068849 Stamp's Mill 1978, 1983, 1985

This small tower mill was built c.1822 and worked by wind until c.1938 and then by engine for a number of years. The cap and two remaining sails were taken off in the early 1950's and it now stands abandoned in a pasture, roofed over and with the doors and windows blocked up. It had four spring shuttered sails, which although they were fixed to a cross in the normal manner were very unusual in this area in being mounted on half stocks, possibly a way of using a set of second-hand sails from a mill fitted with a canister windshaft, or indeed of using existing sails when the old wooden windshaft was replaced. The fantail had been blown off and for many years the mill worked without it, being hand-winded when necessary. There were once four pairs of stones, of which three remain, two French and one grey. The tentering gear is missing, as are the governors, which were mounted directly on the stone spindles. Most of the upper gearing is thought to remain although as access is impossible at present this cannot easily be verified.

41. Freiston TF390428 Freiston Shore 1977

Built in about 1827, this tower mill ceased work by wind in 1924 when the sails were removed, continuing to work by engine for a little while afterwards. It had four patent sails, driving three pairs of stones. The majority of the gear has gone but the wallower, upright shaft and great spur wheel remain. There is also an engine driven hurst on the ground floor. The tower stands disused and derelict with part of the cap frame still lingering in place.

42. Friskney TF481567 Hoyle's Mill 1977

This small tower mill was built at very little expense in the early 19th century using gearing and other items from a dismantled drainage mill. It worked by wind until about 1920 and was then engine-driven for several years. The tower stands capless, used as a store. It had two common and two spring sails, which were removed c.1928 and drove a pair each of French and grey stones. The cap was not the usual ogee type but was gabled and was winded by a braced tailpole, typical of drainage mill practice.

43. Fulstow TF330965 1978 int.

This tower mill was built in the mid 19th century, the precise date being somewhat uncertain. One source gives 1846, another gives 1866-7, while Rex Wailes gives c.1872. Whatever the year, it was erected by Saunderson, the Louth millwright and replaced a post mill. Like all his mills it was finely proportioned and well equipped, although smaller than his large six sail mills. It worked, latterly with two sails, until 1951 when the sails were removed and electric motors installed to drive the machinery. It worked until c.1968 and was demolished in the early 1970's to a stump of little more than one storey, now used as a grain silo. It had four patent sails and was originally fitted with two pairs of French and two pairs of grey stones. Later one pair of French stones was replaced by a roller mill. There was also a mixer.

44. Gainsborough SK822904 Spital Hill 1978

This was one of a pair of tower mills in the same ownership and probably dates from the early 19th century. In 1816 it had five roller reefing sails with three pairs of stones. In about 1870 it was refitted with the patent sails off a mill at Cleethorpes. It worked until 1927 when the sails were removed, and was then allowed to become derelict. It was dismantled in 1976 by David Law who took the machinery to his mill at Horncastle (see below). It now stands derelict with the curb and most of the floors in place. There were four pairs of stones, two French and two grey.

45. Gedney Dyke TF416262 1977 int., 1985

In its prime this was one of the most elegant mills in Lincolnshire. It is dated C.I.R. 1836 and was built for a Mr. Rubbins. It worked until 1942 and lost its six patent sails in 1947. The cap followed soon after and it now stands disused but still in reasonable condition, with most machinery intact. It is very tall, being 68 feet high to the curb, with eight floors. There was a stage at second floor level, and the four pairs of stones remain on the third floor, two French and two grey. It would be tragic if such a fine mill, incomplete though it is, should be lost through neglect or unsympathetic conversion.

46. Gedney Hill TF334116 1977

This tower mill was standing by 1824, and worked by wind until the late 1920's, when the sails were taken off. It was worked by engine until at least the late 1940's, although the cap and top storey had been removed by this time. It is now converted into a house, and has lost all its machinery. There were four patent sails, which drove three pairs of stones.

47. Gosberton TF221301 Risegate 1977 int.

This small tower mill was 'newly erected' in 1824 from which we can assume an early 19th century date. At this time it had a pair of grey and a pair of 'Blue' stones. It was raised and refitted 'lately' in 1853. Rex Wailes gives the date 1840 which is probably the actual date of the rebuild. It worked by wind until 1911 when it was dismantled and altered to its present form. The sails were taken to Helpringham mill, and were patents. Risegate mill is one of only two mills in the county in an unrestored state which retain their windshaft and cross. The cross has lost one of its four arms but is nevertheless of interest, being mounted on the square end of the windshaft with 8 pairs of keys. The original cap has been replaced by a corrugated iron version, similar to the one on Moulton mill. The tower has been gutted and turned into a silo, with a Christy & Norris vertical grinding mill and Bamford crusher on the ground floor, both now disused. The cap frame and windshaft, being such rare survivors, deserve further description. The frame runs on a dead curb, as usual, with the teeth on the upper face outside the track. The neck bearing is outside the cap, the rode baulk being completely exposed. The iron windshaft is 8 inches square across flats at the brakewheel and 9 inches diameter at the neck. The brakewheel has an iron 'spider' (hub and arms) in one piece, with a wooden rim of 7ft. 6in. diameter. An iron tooth ring was bolted on but is now missing. The brake is also of wood and has an exceptionally heavy brake lever. The striking gear at the tail ran on wheels on two guide bars, and had two connecting links to the striking lever.

48. Goxhill (H) TA093208 1978, 1983 int.

Built in 1833, this tower mill worked by wind until the early 1920's, then by engine for a number of years. The sails were removed in 1934 and it was dismantled soon after. The four patent sails drove three pairs of stones. The tower stands disused and is becoming ruinous. All gear has gone except the curb and fragments of the tentering mechanism.

49. Grainthorpe TF382970 1978 int., 1985

Probably dating from the early 19th century, this tower mill originally had roller reefing sails and was hand winded. In 1895 it lost its cap and sails in a tailwind. It was rebuilt, gaining another storey in the process, together with a fantail and four patent sails, the work being done by Saunderson of Louth. It ceased work c.1930 and lost its sails c.1934. There were three pairs of stones. The tower has lost its added top storey and most of the machinery. Part of the wooden upright shaft remains, as do the supports for one of the bedstones, consisting of four iron brackets with levelling screws, an unusual refinement.

50. Grasby TA092051 1978 int.

One of the few post mill fragments to survive, this mill was similar in appearance to those at Wrawby and Burton upon Stather. Little is known about it; it probably dates from the 18th century but as it did not appear at this site until the 1840's was probably moved from elsewhere (the bodily removal of post mills was a fairly common occurence at one time). It worked until just prior to the Great War and was demolished by the early 1920's. A photograph in the Lincolnshire Mill Archive shows it to have had two patent sails. Its internal arrangement is not known, but it is reasonable to expect two pairs of stones to have been carried, probably arranged in the head and tail. The two storeyed roundhouse remains with a scruffy pitched roof and is disused. One crosstree remains in place.

51. Hagworthingham TF344697 1974 int., 1978

This tower mill was standing by 1816, when it had two pairs of stones and common sails. By 1853 it had gained another pair of stones and patent sails, in which form it worked until the early 1940's. The cap and two remaining sails were taken off and a strange roof put on in 1950, since when the tower has fallen into dereliction. All the machinery remained in 1974 although the floors were becoming dangerous. Some smaller items have since been removed and taken to Horncastle mill.

52. Haxey (H) SK761997 1978

Rebuilt in 1823 following a fire, this tower mill worked until early this century, with four patent sails driving three pairs of stones. It was subsequently dismantled and now only the lower two storeys remain, roofed over and used as a store.

16

53. Haxey (H) SE773012 1978 int., 1982 int., 1985

This tower mill was built in 1811 and worked by wind until the 1920s' losing its sails in 1928. It then continued in use with an oil engine. It was eventually refitted with modern machinery, driven by a Ruston & Hornsby diesel engine. It still works to this day and conveys the impression of an old working mill, even if the original plant has been replaced. Originally there were four patent sails, driving three pairs of stones. Later one pair was removed and put on a ground floor hurst to be driven by engine. Stanley Freese visited the mill in 1929 and illustrated its interior in his book 'In Search of English Windmills' (1931). He shows a clasp-arm wooden brakewheel and apparently wallower too; a wooden upper upright shaft with iron lower section, and iron spur gears. A large wooden pulley on the upright shaft drove by belt to a shaft near the wall which drove down to a flour dresser, not shown in the sketch, nor is the sackhoist. Two pairs of stones are shown in place with their tuns, together with a further bedstone. An engine drive is depicted coming up from below the floor to engage with the great spur wheel. A roller mill is also shown, but how this was driven is not apparent; a belt is shown disappearing up to the floor above.

The original cap frame, or part of it, is still in place and the original finial has been incorporated into the later roof although the ball lies on the dust floor. The only other original item to have been kept was the large 'lag' governor, which has now been taken to Bardwell mill in Suffolk, where it is once again carrying out its true function of regulating millstones in a windmill.

54. Haydor SK996387 Oasby Mill 1977 int.

At this tower mill there is an interesting discrepancy over the building date. The tower has a datestone 'R.W.1810'; however an advertisement appeared in 1808 for a new tower mill 'being fitted up'. Perhaps funds ran out and the final completion had to wait for a couple of years. It was originally run in conjunction with a nearby post mill, was subsequently raised and modernised, and worked until 1929. After standing disused for a few years it was dismantled and is now an empty shell. It had four patent sails and four pairs of stones. The tower is beautifully built of ashlar masonry, with the top storey in later brickwork. Unfortunately it was tarred, which masked the fine stonework, although it no doubt helped to keep the mill dry.

55. Heapham SK873887 1978

This tower mill has been plagued by ill fortune in its recent past. It was built by the millwright Johnson of Low Burnham near Haxey in 1876 to replace a post mill. It worked until c.1950 when it was struck by lightning and damaged. Mr. Hewitt, the owner, repaired the mill and set it to work once more, being awarded an S.P.A.B. 'Windmill Certificate' in recognition of his efforts in 1952. Alas, lightning struck again in 1956, this time making a thorough job of wrecking the mill by breaking the iron windshaft in two, dumping the sails on the ground and smashing them to pieces. This time the damage was too great to repair and the mill was abandoned. Some of the gear (two pairs of stones, their fittings and gear) was taken out and put into Heage mill in Derbyshire when that mill was being renovated in 1973. The mill now stands reasonably intact although the cap is going to pieces. There were four patent sails driving three pairs of stones, two French and one grey.

56. Heckington SK145435 Pocklington's Mill 1971 int., 1983, 1985 int.

Known throughout the country as the only remaining eight sail mill, this tower mill's history has also been widely, if at times inaccurately published. It is dated 'MH1830' and was built for Michael Hare by the millwright Edward Ingledew. When first built it had five of Sutton's patent sails, which here were reputed to be 15 feet wide at the tip and 12 feet wide at the heel, with longtitudinal shutters on both sides of the backs, which were 36 feet long. These drove three pairs of stones and in this form the mill worked until 1890 when it fell victim to one of the windmill's most dangerous enemies, a tail-wind. The sails ran backwards and after a short while were blown off completely, taking the entire cap with them, smashing all to pieces. The mill is also reputed to have caught fire in the incident and to have been gutted although this is now believed to have been an error, applying instead to another mill in the village which was burnt out in 1894. At any rate, the mill was a wreck and was abandoned by Mr. Nash, the miller.

This would have been the end of it but for the happy coincidence that the miller at Wyberton mill (see below), John Pocklington, was looking for a suitable mill to fit some mill gear which he had just bought (in 1891) at auction, without having anything specific in mind. The machinery in question was the entire gear, cap, sails etc. from the eight sail mill built in 1813 at Skirbeck, Boston, which was owned and operated at first by Tuxfords, the millwrights and engineers, who no doubt used it as a shining example of their work to show prospective clients around.

During 1891 Mr. Pocklington worked on the refitting of the mill, using direct labour with assistance from the local millwright John Hodgson when necessary. Work was completed in early 1892 and the mill was then set to work, later gaining a large saw-mill on one side, also driven by wind-power. John Pocklington set up a many sided and thriving business combining milling, baking, building and farming. He died in 1941 and the mill ceased work a few years later. It was saved from being dismantled by Kesteven County Council who bought it in 1953 and then restored it as a landmark, replacing four of the sails with two each from Old Bolingbroke and Wainfleet St. Mary mills, the work being done by Thompsons of Alford. Further repairs have been needed from time to time but in 1985 major repairs were put in hand by Lincolnshire County Council, including the construction of 192 new shades and four new sails, with the laudable aim of getting the mill working once more, the work again being entrusted to Thomspons of Alford, with help from the Friends of Heckington Mill.

Heckington mill has eight single-sided patent sails, mounted on a cross which is reputed to weigh five tons. The ogee cap betrays the fact that it is from another mill, being much too large for the tower, but nevertheless it gives the mill a certain elegance. The tips of the sails are linked together by iron rods, an unusual and probably unique refinement, intended to prevent exessive sagging in the sails, although probably unnecessary.

The brakewheel is of timber clasp-arm construction with iron teeth and a wooden brake. It drives an iron wallower on an iron upright shaft. It is thought that only the upper section of the upright shaft, with the wallower, came from Boston, the remainder of the driving gear being original to Heckington. On the third floor, which is the lower of the two bin floors, are two grain cleaners, one a fairly modern Boby driven by electric motor and the other an old separator by Penney and Co, driven by wind. The original three pairs of stones are on the second floor, which also gives access to the stage, driven by an iron great spur wheel and mortice stone nuts. There are two pairs of grey and one pair of French stones and a fourth stone nut takes a drive down to the first floor where there is yet another pair of grey stones. The shaft to this pair utilize spare components including a cunning universal joint above the floor using a quant and mace (the coupling which normally drives the runner stone). At present much of the smaller machinery is damaged although this is being put right by Thompsons during their repairs.

Also on the first floor is the large lag governor which by various cunningly contrived links is able to control all four pairs of stones. At one time a fifth pair of stones, on a ground floor hurst, could also be driven by wind if desired or more usually by engine. There is a mixer on the first floor and there was an elevator from the ground floor as well. An unusual machine is preserved on the first floor; 'Felton's Patent American Grist Mill', made by Riches & Watts of Norwich around the turn of the century. This was tried out but was not a success and so was abandoned. Line shafting formerly took the wind power into the adjoining shed to drive circular and frame saws, but none of this now survives. In a good wind the mill was able to drive all five pairs of stones at the same time and due to its large sail area and well winded site was able to work in very light breezes, when other local mills would have to stand idle.

57. Heckington TF135442 Sleaford Road, Mowbray's Mill 1985

Built stouter than usual, this tower mill was erected in the late 18th or early 19th century and worked until 1931. It was subsequently dismantled and the top storey was removed from the tower, which then received a crenellated top. It now stands empty and disused. There were four patent sails which drove three pairs of stones. There was also a two-pair hurst frame on the ground floor which could be driven by wind or steam.

58. Helpringham TF135405 1971, 1985 int.

This tower mill bears the datestone 'J.B. 1864' and worked by wind until the 1920's, continuing by engine after losing its sails in a gale. The original gear was removed in the 1930's and modern machinery installed. It is still used, now powered by electricity. There were four patent sails driving three pairs of stones on the first floor. Work is now carried out by a combined roller and grinding mill, with an electric sackhoist. The second floor remains virtually the same as when the mill was wind-powered, and on the dust floor some of the old sackhoist remains in place.

59. Hemingby TF241741 1977

Dated 1825, this small tower mill worked until 1911 by wind, when it was converted to engine drive. It continued to work until 1937 when it was burnt out. It was pulled down and the two storey stump re-roofed. It now stands in very poor condition, the bricks having been severely eroded by the weather. It had three pairs of stones, two French and one grey.

60. Hibaldstow (H) SE982028 Reeson's Mill 1978 int., 1983 int., 1985

One of only a handful of such mills, this combines water and wind power in one building. It was built in 1802 near the site of a former post mill. In 1803 it is described as having an 'iron axle' i.e. windshaft and at this time had four common sails. By 1828 two 'regulating' sails had been fitted and four pairs of stones were driven, three French and one grey. In 1837 the windmill was modernised, gaining another storey of brickwork and iron gearing together with patent sails, which were removed in 1913. The water wheel was removed in 1912 when the mill was converted to engine drive, the windmill being abandoned. The cap was taken off, leaving the windshaft and cross resting across the curb. It was eventually taken down in the early 1960's. Milling continued until the mid 1960's when the owners retired. It now stands disused and is in need of some attention, particularly to the tower.

The mill is built on a circular plan, the tower being supported on piers at ground and first floor levels. The outer wall of the watermill is concentric with the tower, except for a flattened portion where the wheel fitted alongside. At first floor level the eight radial dividing walls have vaulted ceilings to support the stage for the windmill above. The windmill tower continues above in stonework for four floors with a brick top floor and attractively corbelled curb. The entrance steps to the watermill consist of a 4 foot 'cullen' or 'blue' stone cut in half. The ground floor was once the spout floor of the watermill and would have contained the driving gears, although how these were arranged cannot now be established accurately. The engine drive enters at this level from an adjacent shed, where latterly an oil engine was installed. This has been removed for restoration by an engine enthusiast. The stairs are unusually ornate and have handrails with balusters. The floor space, like that of the first floor, is rather cluttered because of the radial walls, which produce rather odd-shaped chambers. The first floor was originally the stone floor of the watermill and now contains one pair of grey stones which were overdriven by belt, together with a Bamford combined roller and plate mill. The radial vaulted chambers on this floor were used for various purposes, one containing an old treadle lathe and another containing the miller's office with a desk. Some were used as living accommodation and one still contains a fireplace, the chimney of which emerges above the stage. The second floor is the first in the tower proper and served as both the watermill bin floor and the windmill spout floor. It now contains a pair of grey stones, underdriven by belt. The third floor was the windmill's stone floor and had two pairs of stones, now removed. These were overdriven in the usual manner, the quants and mortice nuts remaining, although not in position. The bridgetree supporting the wooden upright shaft is made from the post mill's crown-tree and looks rather out of place in a tower mill. The great spur wheel is of iron and replaces an earlier wooden wheel. Access above the stone floor is difficult now but much of the gear survives. There is an iron wallower and a later sackhoist, made from parts of an old wire machine. The sixth floor, which was the dust floor, has a concrete deck on it which has fortunately kept the mill dry for the last 60 years or more.

61. Hogsthorpe TF533724 1982

An old mill, this tower was rebuilt or raised in the 19th century. It worked by wind until the early 1920's and then continued by engine until after the last war. It was subsequently dismantled and now only the roofed over single storeyed stump remains, disused and almost completely hidden by dense vegetation. There were four clockwise patent sails, driving three pairs of stones.

62. Holbeach TF358267 Penny Hill 1972, 1983 int., 1985

This tower mill was built in 1826-7 on the site of a smock mill. It originally had four patent sails driving three pairs of stones but in the late 19th century was raised in height by one storey and re-equipped with six patent sails and four pairs of stones. It worked until the late 1930's or early 1940's, latterly on only four sails. By 1953 it had been dismantled and it now stands disused and rapidly falling into decay, there being no roof at present. All the machinery has been removed. Pieces of sails can be seen incorporated into some of the adjoining outbuildings.

63. Horncastle TF266696 Spilsby Road Mill 1977 int., 1982

A very tall tower mill, this was built in 1843, when it had five pairs of stones, three French, one grey and one 'blue'. It worked by wind until 1916 when the sails were removed. The cap followed in the 1920's or early 1930's. It was still worked by oil engine in 1940 but eventually fell into disuse. In 1972 it was purchased by David Law who intended to convert the former stores and engine house into a house and to eventually restore the mill. It had five patent sails and a stage at second floor level with an ornamental handrail. In 1977 the tower was full height with seven storeys but by 1982 the top 14 feet of brickwork had been removed due to its dangerous condition. All that remained of the machinery was the iron lower upright shaft and great spur wheel, together with four pairs of stones, three French and one grey. To fill the gaps the owner acquired the principal gear from Gainsborough mill in 1976, comprising the windshaft with five-arm cross, upright shaft, spur gear and several other items. Other parts have been taken from Hagworthingham mill. At the time of writing the mill is still in its shortened version but rebuilding of the upper portion is due to begin in 1985 or 6. The restoration, being single-handed, is likely to take many years and the owner deserves every encouragement and help in this ambitious project.

64. Horsington TF191683 1982 int.

This little tower mill was built c.1813 and worked until early in the present century. It had been reduced to a stump by 1923 and now stands as a single storeyed stump, roofed over with corrugated iron sheeting. It had four patent sails but the number of stones driven is unknown to me. The brickwork is of rather poor quality and the walls are only 1½ bricks (14 inches) thick, even at ground floor level.

65. Huttoft TF514767 1982

This once elegant tower mill was built in the early or mid 19th century; two dates are quoted by different sources, 1826 and c.1844. A large steam mill was erected in 1872 and the windmill worked until gale damage forced its retirement in 1945. It was then gutted and converted into a grain silo. The cap lingered for a number of years, being taken off at the same time as the one on Addlethorpe mill in 1968. The tower still retains its fine wrought iron stage which is almost identical with one on Sibsey mill, suggesting that Saunderson of Louth may have had a hand in the mill at some time. The mill used to be painted grey which made a change from the more usual tar; since ceasing work it has gained a coat of tar however. There were four patent sails, working four pairs of stones, two French and two grey.

66. Ingham SK942836 1978

Built for a Mr. Ellis in 1872 for £1000, this tower mill only worked for a short while, being disused by 1923. It lingered as a derelict for a short while but was eventually gutted and was converted into a house in the 1960's. There were four patent sails but the number of stones driven is unknown to me.

67. Kirton TF289402 Kirton End 1977

Erected in 1833 to replace a post mill, this tower mill worked by wind until c.1936 when the sails were removed, continuing by engine for a number of years after this. The cap was taken off in the 1960's and the tower now stands disused. The machinery was also removed in the 1960's, only the three pairs of stones (two grey and one French) remaining. There were four patent sails. In 1975 the owners stated their intention to restore the mill but whether this will ever come about remains to be seen.

68. Kirton in Lindsey (H) SK939994 Mount Pleasant Mill 1978, 1985 int.

This is another of the tower mills that have been erected on top of a post mill roundhouse, although here the junction is so subtle as to be almost indistinguishable. It is only given away by the fact that the walls begin vertically at ground level, with smaller bricks and thicker tar than the remainder of the mill, which is built in large 3 inch machine moulded bricks laid to the batter of the tower. Over the door is the inscription 'E.L. 1875' recording the date of this transformation. It worked by wind until 1936 and then continued by engine until 1973, worked by Fred Banks together with the mill at Alford. It was then acquired by Alan Turner who has established a thriving railway and milling museum at the site, and who now works the mill on special open days by portable steam engine. The mill is open to the public and there are plans to restore the cap and sails. This mill and the one at Heapham have the only unrestored caps in the county. Here the fanstage has been removed, but all the parts have been preserved on site since the 1930's and are in excellent condition. The cap frame is of oak and the windshaft is of cast iron, with a four-armed cross to take the patent sails once fitted. The brakewheel is of timber clasp arm construction with an iron tooth ring and a wooden brake. The wallower is iron, as are the upright shaft and great spur wheel. The sackhoist is worked off the underside of the wallower by a friction ring, as is the usual practice in the area. The dust floor beams, amongst others, are re-used from an old post mill at Wrawby and still have tar on them. The bin floor beams have been replaced with laminated beams made from three planks bolted together vertically and are very unusual in a windmill. The stones were on the second floor and of the original three pairs only one pair of greys remain, over-driven by a mortice stone nut on a quant. The meal spout passes right through the first floor to emerge at ground floor level, a modification to tie in with the engine-driven hurst on the ground floor. This is iron-framed, by Marshall Sons & Co. Ltd. of Gainsborough and has a pair of grey stones fitted with 'silent feed' instead of the more usual 'damsel'. The single governor is on the first floor and acts on the iron bridgetree, only one of which remains in place. The engine drive enters at just above ground level and drives the hurst as well as the remainder of the mill by means of a shaft engaging the great spur wheel. An unusual refinement is the elevator to replace the old sackhoist and the elevator to feed the first floor bin for the hurst.

Until 1984 there was the roof of a post mill near the mill, used as a shed. This may have come from the original mill here but is more likely to have come from another post mill to the south of the village. It had become very derelict by 1984 and to save it from total destruction it was recorded, then dismantled and taken to Skidby mill near Hull where the gable has been reconstructed and put on display at the mill museum there.

69. Langton TF244694 1977

Built in 1861 by C. Clark of Horncastle to replace a post mill, this tower mill worked until 1936 when the sails were damaged and had to be removed. It was eventually dismantled and the tower now stands in a modern farming complex, used as a store. It had four patent sails, driving three pairs of stones, two grey and one French. It also retained a smutter and flour machine into the 1930's, the latter especially being a rare survival.

70. Leadenham SK921532 Lowfield Mill 1977 int.

One of a pair of mills, both towers, this was built in 1840 to replace a post mill and in 1841 various spare parts from this were sold, including four 'roller reefing' sails and a pair of 'black' (or 'cullen') stones. The second mill had gone by the turn of the century but the remaining one worked until about 1930. It eventually lost its cap but the tower retained all its gear until the early 1980's when the stones were taken to Sneinton mill, Nottingham together with gearing and other parts, to be used in the restoration of 'Green's Mill'. The wire machine, one of the last to remain in the county, was taken to Bardwell, Suffolk in 1984 where it is now being put to good use again in a windmill. All that remains in the mill now is the smutter.

The machinery as inspected in 1977 comprised two pairs of French and one pair of grey stones; the lower part of the upright shaft and the remains of the great spur wheel, both iron; the quants and mortice stone nuts; the power take-off for the auxiliary machines, all on the second floor; a smutter (reel type) and wire machine, both quite large machines, mounted under the first floor.

71. Legbourne TF362842 1978

Like Hibaldstow mill, this is a combined wind and water mill. Here however, the combination was complete as the three pairs of stones could be driven either by wind or water power. It was built in 1847 by Saunderson of Louth on an existing water mill site and worked by wind until the mid 1920's, carrying on by water for a while after this. It was eventually gutted and converted into a house. The stage has been retained, as has the external iron breastshot wheel, formerly enclosed in a wheel house. It had four patent sails which drove the stones overdrift in the usual manner. The wheel drove the same stones underdrift, with duplicated spur gearing. The upright shaft was not continuous however as it was not practical to have both drives engaged at once.

72. Lincoln SK971722 Mill Road, Ellis' Mill 1977 int., 1978 int., 1983 int., 1985

This very small tower mill was built in 1798. It was eventually equipped with patent sails and worked until 1941 when one of the remaining pair of sails was blown off. The cap was taken off in the 1940's, followed by the machinery. The tower then stood disused until 1975, when it was set on fire and completely gutted. This would have been the end of it but for the timely intervention of Lincoln Civic Trust, who set about the rebuilding of the mill as a 'Silver Jubilee' project in 1977 using some professional labour and some unemployed young people on a 'Job Creation' scheme. Chris Salisbury was in charge of the main project with Thompson's employed to sort out the machinery and build the sails and fantail. The cap was built during 1978 and the mill was completed during 1980. It ground for the first time on 26 April 1981 and since then has been regularly run for visitors by volunteer millers, led by Barry Brooke.

The restoration was made possible because second-hand machinery was available from other mills; a latter-day Heckington in effect. The upright shaft, stones (one pair French and one pair grey), spur gearing and tentering gear came from Toynton All Saints mill which was due to be gutted and house converted, thus putting this machinery to good use. The windshaft and brake wheel, a very fine iron example, came from Sturton by Stow mill, where all the other gear was missing so what remained was again being put to good use. In return, a replica cap in glassfibre was made for Sturton mill which thereby benefitted from the deal.

The new cap is very much more bulbous than the original which did not have the reverse curve now on the petticoat. The fantail was originally mounted further out and the sails were originally much bigger, being real 'daisy cutters'. To protect visitors it was decided to make the sails shorter and to preserve the correct proportions the width was cut down to match. The resulting sails are not as powerful as they once were but as the mill does not have to rely on them for a living to any great extent the sacrifice is worthwhile.

The mill is a credit to the people of Lincoln, and makes a lovely sight when approaching the city from the West. It also presents a tantalising glimpse of patent sails and cap to travellers on the city ring road, which it towers above. Finding it by road can be more difficult, the best course of action being to follow signs to the Museum of Lincolnshire Life in Burton Road (itself worth a visit, and home of the Lincolnshire Mill Archive). Mill Road is parallel to Burton Road and the mill stands behind the museum somewhat incongruously amongst the rows of terraced houses.

73. Lincoln SK971703 Princess Street, LeTall's Mill 1977 int., 1985

Built by the Seeley family, this huge tower mill was erected in the late 1840's as a five sail mill with four pairs of stones, three French and one grey. It was acquired by Henry LeTall in 1871 when it is said to have had six sails, although another source suggests that the sails were taken off in 1860, steam being the motive power after this. Millstones were used at the mill, which grew in size extensively, until 1888, when roller flour mills were put in by Joseph Thornton, millwright of Retford. The mill tower was then gutted and converted into a silo and water tower, in which form it survives to this day. Flour is no longer made at the mill, which has gone over to making animal feedstuffs. The future of the premises is uncertain however and there are plans to develop the area for housing. The mill tower, which at 77 feet 6 inches high to the curb (which still remains), is the second highest in the county, indeed probably the country, will hopefully be retained in any redevelopment for it is an imposing sight towering over the cluttered terraced houses at its base. There are, or rather were, nine floors, with an iron reefing stage (which remains) at fifth floor level. The internal diameter at ground floor level is 28 feet 10 inches and at the curb is 11 feet.

74. Long Sutton TF440221 Brunswick Mill 1971, 1977, 1985

This rather sad-looking tower mill was until quite recently one of the 'best' derelict mills in the county. It was built in 1817 when it had four sails and was about five storeys high. In the mid 19th century it was raised in height by another floor, this being done so well that it is hard to tell the later work from the original. It was refitted with six patent sails, which drove three pairs of stones (originally two French and one grey, but later two grey and one French). It ceased work in the 1930's and was then allowed to remain derelict and disused. The cap was blown off c.1963 and following an occasion when the sails rotated in a gale, shedding pieces of wood as they went, the owner removed the sails, windshaft and cap frame by crane on 15 August 1973. It had once been hoped to restore the mill but the scrap value of the iron machinery proved irresistable and most went to be melted down in the furnaces at Scunthorpe. The sails and cap frame were burned in a huge bonfire and the now decrepit tower has been left to decay, still containing some of its machinery. This was the most recent of many such acts of vandalism in the cause of 'safety' and hopefully in these more enlightened times will be the last in the county. The loss of a mill as outwardly complete as this is regretable to say the least, but it must be said that by 1971 the cap frame and sails were, on close inspection, beyond repair, making any restoration a costly affair.

75. Long Sutton TF438228 Harrison's Mill 1971, 1985 int.

This tower mill was built for Charles Treffitt in 1843 and thanks to a local man's diary we know when construction began to the day, namely 17 February. It worked until the 1920's by wind after which it ran by engine for a number of years. The six sails were taken off in the 1930's and were reputedly put on Brunswick mill. It was eventually gutted for its ironwork and abandoned to its fate. It now stands disused and derelict with most of the floors in place. The present owners hope to conserve it and if possible to improve it. All that remains of the machinery is the wooden upper upright shaft together with bits and pieces of tentering gear and the remains of a hurst on the ground floor. It had six patent sails driving three pairs of stones on the first floor. It is said to have ended its days with five pairs of stones, but where the other two were is now difficult to establish; possibly the ground floor hurst had two pairs.

76. Luddington (H) SE828174 1978 int.

This early 19th century tower mill worked until early this century, losing its sails in 1929. It was eventually dismantled and pulled down to its present two storeyed stump in the 1950's. All that remains of the machinery is the three bedstones on the first floor, two French and one grey.

77. Ludford Magna TF200895 1978 int.

This now rather inauspicious stump has the distinction of being the remains of the last new windmill to be built in Lincolnshire. It was built in 1889 by Saunderson and worked for a short time only, ceasing work by wind in about 1930. The sails were taken off by 1932 and the tower was reduced to its present two storeyed stump after the war. It is now used as a grain silo.

78. Lutton TF436243 Lutton Gowts, Sneath's Mill 1971 int., 1982 int., 1985.

The oldest complete tower mill in the county, this mill is dated 'T.D. Ayliff 1779' on a large stone, said to have been a sundial. The mill is like no other left in the county and resembles a brick-built smock mill, even to the extent of being octagonal in plan. It worked until the early 1930's and was then abandoned. Attempts were made in 1939 to secure its preservation but unfortunately the war intervened and nothing was ever done. By 1971 only part of one sail remained and the cap was missing. The decay has since accelerated sharply; the sail has gone and the cap frame is breaking up while the floors are ready to collapse. Attempts are being made to at least conserve what remains and in late 1985 some of the parts were removed by crane as a prelude to restoration by Long Sutton Civic Trust. The mill has a wooden windshaft with an iron poll end and clasp arm brakewheel. The clasp arm wallower is cogged in a very crude and old-fashioned manner, being a 'trundle' or face gear wheel. All the upper machinery has suffered badly from exposure to the elements. The upright shaft is wooden, with a clasp arm great spur wheel. The stone nuts, stones and tentering gear are all missing, but two pairs were fitted, one French and one grey. The drive to the flour dresser is largely intact and is mostly of wood, driven by a pinion from the great spur wheel. The machine itself is also missing. One millstone remains where it fell, on the ground floor.

The mill had a simple cap with triangular gables and a straight ridge, turned to wind by means of a braced tailpole and winch. A weathercock was fitted above the rear gable. The sails were carried on stocks and comprised a pair of common and a pair of spring shuttered sails.

79. Maltby le Marsh TF470820 1978, 1985 int.

Yet another of the mills built by Saunderson of Louth, this little tower mill was erected in 1841 and worked by wind until 1952, and then by engine for a few more years. Like many mills in the county it then fell victim to scrap collectors and was gutted.

A change for the better occurred in the early 1980's as a replica cap made of glassfibre has been fitted, enhancing its appearance. Some form of domestic conversion is likely to take place eventually, which will at least preserve the tower, which is completely stripped of ironwork, even the curb having gone. The stones were taken out by Thompsons in 1978 for use in other mills and all that remains now is the wooden upright shaft. Four patent sails drove three pairs of stones.

80. Mareham le Fen TF281610 1978 int.

The strangest of all the surviving mills in the county from a structural viewpoint, this presents a good example of how **not** to build a tower mill. It was originally built in, or shortly before, 1820. At some later date it was decided to raise it in height by two storeys. The tower had very little 'batter' or slope, being nearly vertical, so the raising was achieved by inserting a parallel section of two floors in the **middle** of the tower, instead of at the top, as was usually the practice. How this was achieved can only be guessed at; in theory it would have been possible to jack up the top of the tower, building on new courses to plug the gap as work progressed, or a more severe rebuilding may have been employed. At any rate, the mill ended up six floors in height with a ground floor diameter of little more than the curb, which was generously corbelled out. The not entirely surprising result was that the puny tower began to crack up at the base. Another strange piece of work was then applied to remedy the situation; the lower two floors were encased in another 'skin' of brickwork laid in simple stretcher bond with no apparent attempt to bond in with the existing work. It has to be said however that the tower has survived reasonably well for all its defects, but it cannot be said to be one of the county's finest, when compared to mills such as Moulton or East Kirkby.

The four patent sails are thought to have been removed in the 1910's, engine power being used after this. The cap was removed in 1939 and probably by this time all the original gear had gone. The tower stands disused and contains later power-driven gear comprising a pair of grey stones on a hurst, a mixer on the first floor and a sackhoist on the second floor.

81. Marsh Chapel TF362993 1978 int.

This little tower mill replaced a post mill in 1835 and worked until gale damage forced its retirement in about 1908. It now stands to just below curb level in good condition and is used as a store. The foundations must be quite shallow for it has developed a pronounced lean. Three pairs of stones were driven and a rather indistinct old photograph shows two double sided patent sails and what appear to be two roller reefing sails. No fantail is visible and it is likely that it was hand-winded by means of a wheel and endless chain although these are not visible in the picture.

82. Marton SK834816 1978 int., 1985.

This tiny tower mill on the bank of the Trent was in existence by 1799. It drove two pairs of stones, one French and one grey. In 1853 it had two common and two spring sails but it finished with four patent sails. It was dismantled completely in 1927 and now stands as a shell. Part of the cap frame remained in 1978 but this has now gone. There is a fireplace on the ground floor. Some repairs had been carried out to the brickwork by 1985.

83. Metheringham TF064613 1977

One of the group of tall six sail mills once to be found in the county this is dated 'H.B.1867'. It seems to have not enjoyed much prosperity later on because as each sail was lost it was not replaced, the other ones being juggled around to maintain the balance. It ran therefore with the intriguing sequence of 6, then 4, then 2 and finally 3 sails, in which form it finished work in the 1920's or early 1930's. It stood until 1942 with three sails and due to its bizarre (and possibly unique) appearance was the frequent subject of visits by mill enthusiasts during the 1920's and 30's and is one of the most photographed mills in the county. As late as 1961 the cap frame and windshaft were still in place but these have now gone. Access is difficult so at present it is impossible to establish the condition of the interior, although most of the machinery is thought to remain. Now that the tar is wearing off the tower it is possible to see the unusual banding in the brickwork. The iron reefing stage remains in bad condition at second floor level, having been swiped by various sails at intervals as they crashed to the ground. As previously stated, six patent sails were carried. The brakewheel and all the gearing was of iron and four pairs of stones were driven. The mill is now disused and is becoming derelict.

84. Middle Rasen TF091888 1978

Standing by 1827, this tower mill had two pairs of stones, one French and one grey. At some time it was raised by another storey and it worked until the 1920's by wind, losing its sails by 1931, when it was engine-driven. When the last miller died in 1932 it became disused and was subsequently dismantled. There were four patent sails. The tower has lost the top portion and is now at about the height it began its life with. It was disused until 1985 but is now to be made into part of a commercial premises established in the adjoining buildings.

85. Morton SK810921 1978

This tower mill is stated by Rex Wailes to have been built in 1820 and it was already disused by 1918. All that now remains is the shell standing five storeys high behind laundry premises.

86. Moulton TF307240 1972, 1977 int., 1982 int.

This colossal tower mill has the distinction of being the largest surviving windmill not only in Lincolnshire, but in the whole country. It cannot claim to be the largest complete windmill, that honour falling to Sutton mill in Norfolk, which is 80 feet high to the top of its cap. Moulton mill however is 80 feet high to the curb and was originally about 97 feet high to the top of its ogee cap. It was built in about 1822 by Robert King. The sails were removed in 1895 after gale damage, when a steam mill with a two sack Turner roller milling plant was installed in the adjoining granary, steam power also being applied to the original stones. Serious milling ceased many years ago although a small roller mill and kibbler probably see occasional use. The main use of the mill now is as a store in connection with the grain merchant's business of Mr. Biggadike, whose family have owned the mill since 1924.

The tower is 28 feet 9 inches in diameter at ground level and 12 feet diameter at the curb, both internally. The basement contains the engine drive gearing which then ascends to the great spur wheel by way of a vertical shaft. The elevated ground floor is spacious enough to contain a proper partitioned miller's office. The first floor contains a Turner 'Inkoos' mill (or kibbler) and Hunt's roller mill, both electrically powered. The second floor has large storage bins. The third floor was the spout floor; unfortunately the governor has gone. Access to the reefing stage, now missing, was formerly at this level; the two door openings have been partly bricked up. The three pairs of stones are on the fourth floor. Two pairs of French stones remain in place with their vats; one pair are 4'6" and one pair are 4'4", the latter having the plate around the eye 'W.J.&T.CHILD.MAKER.HULL.1853'. The pair of grey stones are 4'8" diameter and have been taken up, now leaning against the wall.

The spur gearing differs from the usual Lincolnshire pattern in that the stone nuts are all iron, the great spur wheel having morticed wooden cogs. This arrangement is fine until a breakage, when the job of re-cogging would take several weeks. The spur wheel has an iron hub and rim, with eight radial wooden spokes. The cogs are of very fine pitch and are very wide, which must have given a very smooth drive. The engine drive engages the spur wheel by means of another small iron nut. The nuts are 12 inches in diameter and the great spur wheel is 8'9" in diameter.

The fifth and sixth floors both contain bins, the seventh is empty and eighth is the dust floor. The wallower is an impressive wooden clasp-arm bevel wheel of about 6 feet in diameter with wooden cogs. A friction rim on the underside formerly drove the endless chain sackhoist, now displaced in favour of an electric hoist. The upright shaft is of wood and is 14 inches square. It changes to iron of 5½ inches diameter just above the spur wheel.

The curb is a hexagonal wooden frame built into the brickwork, with an iron track and an inward facing tooth ring, beneath which the centring wheels run. The cap frame is in poor condition but survives mostly intact apart from where the sheertrees have been cut off beyond the new roof (fitted in 1928 to replace the old ogee cap). The windshaft has gone but the tail bearing housing remains, as does the hand winding gear. Parts of the brakewheel also remain in the basement.

The mill had four double sided patent sails, which unusually for Lincolnshire were carried on stocks in a poll end. The fanstage was of the typical local type with the rear fly posts almost vertical. Apart from the loss of its windshaft and original roof, the mill is remarkably complete and is well cared for at present. It is certainly a viable candidate for full restoration, but whether or not this can ever be achieved remains to be seen.

87. Moulton TF294182 Moulton Chapel 1973, 1983 int.

Built in 1865 to replace a post mill, this tower mill worked until about 1930 by wind and then by engine for a number of years. The sails were taken off in about 1938 after gale damage and it was later largely dismantled. It was driven by electricity in the 1950's but eventually went into disuse. It is now undergoing gradual house conversion by its owner. The only gear to survive is one pair of grey stones, with the stone nut replaced by a pulley. There were two pairs of grey stones and one pair of French stones, together with another pair of grey stones on a ground floor hurst, engine-powered. The tower has lost about 4 feet in height but still contains all the floors and it is in these that most of the mill's interest lies. The fourth floor beams are the tarred oak sheers of the old post mill, with clear wear marks visible where the post and collar rubbed; the fifth floor beams are cut from an old stock, still with its white paint on.

88. North Hykeham SK940656 1977

This tower mill seems to have been erected between 1824 and 1830 and worked until c.1925. It was dismantled almost immediately and was reduced to a two storeyed stump. By 1977 this was just a derelict shell about 12 feet high but in the early 1980's it was converted into a summer-house, in the process gaining a beautifying layer of mock stone cladding. There were four patent sails.

89. North Kelsey TA036013 'New Mill' 1978

This tower mill was built in the early 19th century and had fallen into disuse by 1905. No details of its machinery have come to hand. The tower stands to its full height and is disused. A conical roof was fitted but this is now in disrepair.

90. Old Leake TF398521 Leake Commonside, Howsam's Mill 1977 int.

Built in 1859, this tower mill worked, latterly in an increasingly tatty state until 1950, when the sails and cap, together with the top 3 or 4 feet of brickwork were removed. Work continued by engine power, eventually being superceded by electricity and modern milling machinery, which was still in use in 1977. Some old machinery remains, comprising the lower iron upright shaft and iron great spur wheel, the governor and four bedstones, two French and two grey. There were four double sided patent sails.

91. Owston Ferry (H) SK815992 1978

One of three tower mills on the bank of the Trent at Owston Ferry, this was probably built in the early 19th century and had gone out of use by 1923. By 1934 it had been dismantled and reduced to a three storeyed stump, in which form it remains, disused. There were four patent sails and three pairs of stones.

92. Pelham's Lands TF208539 Chapel Hill (near Dogdyke) 1977

This tower mill carried the datestone 'L.S.1838' and was built to replace a post mill which had been blown down. It lost its cap in 1926 after which it was engine-driven. There were four patent sails which drove three pairs of stones. It was eventually partly demolished and only the derelict single storeyed stump remains.

93. Pickworth TF042342 1977

This small tower mill was built by the millwright Ingledew to replace a post mill in the early 19th century. It ceased work early this century and was later used as a cheese factory. The tower was still at its full height in the 1940's but it has now been reduced to a two storeyed stump and appears to be used as a store. There were two common and two spring sails driving a pair of French and a pair of grey stones.

94. Pinchbeck TF227260 Northgate Mill 1977

Built in 1848 to replace a post mill, this tower mill worked until 1922 by wind, carrying on by engine for a number of years afterwards. It was gutted in the mid 1930's and is now used for storage in connection with the modern mill in the adjacent buildings. It had four patent sails and drove four pairs of stones.

95. Pinchbeck TF206252 Glenside 1977

This little tower mill is dated 'R.T.1812' and was built using the principal gearing from an old marsh mill in Bourne Fen. It was raised by another storey at some stage and worked by wind until 1931. The last pair of sails were damaged by a gale and were removed in 1932 or 3. It was dismantled c.1945, continuing to work using modern milling machinery driven by engine. It remained in use until the late 1970's. There were four spring sails mounted on stocks in a poll end, which drove two pairs of stones. The tower has developed a serious lean over the years and one side is now almost vertical.

96. Ropsley and Humby SK991340 Ropsley Mill 1977

Built in the mid 19th century, this tower mill worked until early this century by wind. It then ran by engine power for a number of years but was partly demolished in the late 1950's or early 60's. The two storeyed stump remains as a store amongst farm buildings. There were four patent sails, driving four pairs of stones.

97. Saxilby SK892748 1978 int.

This tower mill was built in 1823 and ceased to work by wind in the 1920's. The sails were removed in 1927 but it carried on by engine for a number of years. The cap had been removed by 1931 and the mill now stands disused. There were four patent sails and a steam engine with a very tall chimney adjoining the mill. Much of the machinery has survived; the upright shaft has a square wooden upper section and an iron lower section with an iron wallower and great spur wheel. The friction-driven sackhoist remains, as do two pairs of grey and one pair of French stones. The quants, stone nuts and tentering gear have all been removed.

98. Scawby (H) SE 972058 1978, 1985

There was a 'newly erected' flour mill advertised here in 1829 when it had two pairs of stones. The surviving tower shows that it was raised at some stage. It has been out of use since at least 1908 and is now an empty shell, not quite to its full height. There were four patent sails.

99. Scopwick TF058576 1977 int.

This once fine, tall tower mill was built in 1827 and was later raised by one storey, probably when it gained an adjoining steam mill in 1842. It worked until 1912 and was dismantled soon afterwards. The steam mill became derelict and was demolished but the tower has been allowed to remain and is an empty shell. There were four patent sails, driving three pairs of stones, with a further three pairs in the steam mill.

100. Scotter SE883005 Cottingham's Mill 1978

Built to replace a post mill in 1874 by the millwright Hett, of Brigg, this tower mill worked until the late 1930's and after a period of dereliction was dismantled. It had four patent sails, which drove two pairs of grey and one pair of French stones. The tower now stands disused, with the top two storeys removed. One bedstone is said to remain, but otherwise all the machinery has been removed.

101. Scremby TF438684 Grebby Mill 1977 int., 1985

This once attractive tower mill is dated 'I.E.1812' and replaced a post mill. It was worked in its latter days by Dobson's in conjunction with their mill at Burgh le Marsh. By 1946 only two sails remained and work finally ceased in late 1949. The last pair of sails were taken to Cross in Hand post mill in Sussex where they were converted to fit a stock and continued to work until 1969. The cap and ironwork were taken away c.1963 after which it was allowed to stand derelict. In 1977 the tower stood intact with the wooden upright shaft, two pairs of grey and one pair of French stones. The grey stones have now been taken to Burgh mill and the tower has been converted into a house, gaining a large addition to one side and a rather odd 'cap'. A large datestone '1983' has been tastelessly inserted into the tower to record this transformation. In 1985 the mill and house were incomplete and unoccupied.

102. Scunthorpe (H) SE902113 1978, 1983, 1985 int.

Erected in 1858 to replace a post mill, this nicely proportioned tower mill worked until 1917 when the miller, Mr. Long, was blinded by a German incendiary bomb which dropped nearby. It had been dismantled by the late 1930's and until 1982 was used as a store. In the late 1970's the possibility of restoring the mill was contemplated and machinery taken from Brook's mill, Epworth, was earmarked for the project. As events turned out the project was never initiated and the tower was converted to offices initially. The only restoration work carried out was the construction of an excellent replica ogee cap by students of the Construction Department, North Lindsey College of Technology with financial help from Mr. J.D. Tighe and Scunthorpe Borough Council. The cap carries a dummy cross but unfortunately no rode balk has been fitted, which leaves the windshaft mysteriously suspended. In 1984 the adjoining buildings were converted into a public house, and the former spout floor of the mill is now a lounge, with a particularly interesting ceiling consisting of two French and one grey bedstone, one with its stone spindle in place. In the wall of the bar is a grey runner stone which has had the old-fashioned type of four-armed rhynd and outside are another pair of grey stones carrying a plaque recording the project's history.

103. Sibsey TF344510 Trader Mill 1978, 1982, 1985 int.

In my opinion this is the best looking of all the Lincolnshire tower mills, although I also believe that Alford mill has the best internal arrangement. The mill was built by Saunderson of Louth in 1877 to replace a small post mill, and what a difference the miller must have noticed when he first used his new mill! It is not exceptionally tall, containing only six floors above ground and the height to the top of the cap is 74 feet 3 inches. However the slenderness of the tower and the flat landscape in which it stands create the impression that it is bigger than it really is, and make the (admittedly large) sails look enormous in proportion.

It worked until 1954, latterly with four sails and was then allowed to become derelict. It was later taken over by the Department of the Environment who restored it in 1970 to 'static' condition. In 1981 they got the mill into full working order with Thompsons of Alford employed to make the hundreds of shutters needed and to get the fantail working. Several curb segments were replaced and the old ones remain on the ground, allowing an opportunity for detailed examination, usually denied.

The ground floor is now virtually empty but originally contained a hurst driven by engine from an adjoining shed. The elevator which formerly fed this remains and terminates in a hopper on the first floor. One spout passes down to the ground floor.

The first floor contains the tentering gear and spouts. The second floor gives access to the very ornate iron stage and contains the three remaining pairs of stones of the four pairs originally fitted. There are two pairs of grey stones and one pair of French. The grey runner stones have both been backed with concrete to increase their weight, a sure sign of a hard working life. The great spur wheel is of iron on an iron upright shaft and drives through mortice stone nuts. The third and fourth floors are both bin floors although no bins actually remain, merely holes in the floor. The fifth floor is the dust floor and contains the iron sackhoist with an endless chain. The brake wheel and wallower are of iron, as are the brake and brake lever.

Power is provided by six double sided patent sails. At present the mill is not worked, although it could do with little or no preparation. It is hoped to allow it to run on special open days but meanwhile it remains open to the public.

104. Sibsey TF352514 Rhoade's Mill 1978

This tower mill was standing by 1823 and was at some stage raised by another storey. It ceased work in 1921 and in 1924 the sails and fantail were taken off. The cap had gone by 1934 and in this form the tower remains as a store with no machinery remaining. There were two pairs of stones and at one time it was driven by 'Bywater's roller reefing sails' which used longitudinal rollers clothing the whole length of the sail in one go.

105. Skidbrooke with Saltfleet Haven TF456936 Saltfleet Mill 1978, 1983 int.

Now sadly derelict, this tower mill is one of the oldest in the county and stands on the old sea bank on a slightly raised mound. It is said to be dated 1770 although I was unable to find evidence of this. It originally had one pair of French, one pair of grey and one pair of cullen stones and was driven by four roller reefing sails. The cap was hand-winded, originally by braced tailpole, later by wheel and chain. In the 1890's it was largely rebuilt, gaining a vertical extension in height of more than one storey, a new cap, fantail and four patent sails. Possibly at this time the old ground floor which was partly below ground level was abandoned, the first floor becoming a new raised lower floor. Work continued until about 1951, latterly with very tatty sails which were removed about this time. It was subsequently pulled to pieces, much of the ironwork being taken for scrap. It now stands completely derelict and disused although there is a possibility of house conversion at some future date which would at least preserve the structure.

The remains of the cap frame and sails still lie where they fell. In the ceiling of the ground floor can be seen a small smutter and the engine drive gearing. On the first floor remain three pairs of stones, two French and one grey, together with the lower iron upright shaft and the iron great spur wheel. A small pulley just above the footstep bearing once drove the governor. The engine drive shaft and its mortice nut remain but the stone nuts are missing, as are virtually all the floors above this level. There is a fireplace on the present ground floor and an old ship's mast helps to support the stone floor.

106. Sleaford TF069456 Money's Mill 1977, 1983, 1985

This huge tower mill was in existence by 1798, being depicted in an engraving of that date as having a broad reefing stage, squat ogee cap with fantail and four common sails. It was probably not very old at this time and it was subsequently rebuilt or modernised c.1810, when it was also raised slightly. It worked until 1895 when the miller became bankrupt and the mill was subsequently dismantled. There were three pairs of stones and it formerly had large buildings attached to its base. The tower stands to its full height of approaching 70 feet, with eight storeys and is at present disused, although there are plans to preserve it, probably involving some kind of conversion. All that remained of the machinery was a power drive from below to the spur wheel, but this was removed in 1985 during preliminary conversion work.

107. South Rauceby TF024457 1977

This tower mill is dated 'I.G.R.1841' and worked by wind until the early 1930's, continuing by engine for a while after this. It was gutted and converted into a house in the 1940's and in this form remains today. There were four patent sails driving three pairs of stones, two grey and one French. A further two pairs could be driven by engine. The stones were on the second floor which formerly possessed a stage. The lower part of the iron upright shaft and the iron great spur wheel remain.

108. Spalding TF234201 Spalding Common 1977

Built in about 1816, this tower mill worked by wind until 1934. The sails were taken off in 1939 and the upper part of the mill was taken down in 1943, leaving the two storeyed stump which is now in rather derelict condition. There were four patent sails driving the two pairs of French and one pair of grey stones. The cap, like other mills in the area, was particularly bulbous and the tower had a very pronounced lean, another common feature of Fenland mills!

109. Stallingborough (H) TA191106 1983

Dated 'A.D.1875', this mill replaced an earlier tower, even using some of its parts like the curb, which was too small for the new mill. It worked, latterly in rough mechanical order, until 1954. It was the awful state of the fan gearing which let it down for it stopped turning to wind and suffered a tailwinding, losing the sails, windshaft, brakewheel and half the cap. It was then abandoned and was gutted in the 1960's when it became a house. There were four patent sails, driving three pairs of stones on the stone floor with a further two pairs on the floor below.

110. Stickford TF346589 1978, 1985

This small tower mill is dated 'R.Kyme 1820' and worked until 1952, latterly in an amazingly bad state of repair. It ran for the last few years with the cap stuck in one direction and was therefore only able to work when the wind blew from that quarter. It stood derelict until the late 1960's when the sails were removed and the windshaft was taken to Morcott mill in Rutland which was rebuilt as a house. This was a great shame as the mill was in a very complete state, albeit very derelict. It was thankfully covered over to protect it from the worst of the weather and stands today in a derelict state, but complete internally. The cap frame is still in place and the old sails still lie at the foot of the tower. There are plans to conserve the mill and maybe to restore it eventually. There were four patent sails, driving one pair of French and one pair of grey stones.

111. Stickney TF345569 1978, 1985

Built in 1842 for William Balderston, this tower mill worked until 1952 when as a new cap was required, which the owners couldn't afford, it was dismantled and fitted with modern electric machinery. Work ceased finally in the late 1960's and the tower is now used as a store in connection with an engineering works. There were four patent sails driving three pairs of stones on the second floor, two grey and one French, with a further pair of greys on the first floor driven by engine.

112. Sturton by Stow SK881804 1978, 1985

This tower mill was built in 1815 as a 'subscription mill'. It worked until the early 1950's, losing its sails in late 1954. It was gutted in the late 50's but the cap was left in place, allowing the restorers of Lincoln mill to obtain a new windshaft and brakewheel for their mill from here in 1978. Part of the deal was to reinstate the cap so a fibreglass replica was made and fitted that year. It is not quite the same shape as the original but improves the tower's appearance nevertheless. No machinery remains but the tower is preserved. There were four patent sails, driving one pair of grey and two pairs of French stones.

113. Sutterton TF273359 1973, 1985

Described as being 'newly erected' in 1855 this mill is thought to date from the 1840's. It worked by wind until 1921 when the sails were removed. It then stood derelict for a while, still retaining its cap frame and windshaft in 1942, although the stones had gone by this time. It now stands as a capless tower and is disused. There were four patent sails driving three pairs of stones, with another pair engine driven on the ground floor.

114. Sutton on Sea TF503807 Sutton Ings 1982 int.

This tiny tower mill is a very rare survival indeed, the last of its type in the county and one of only a handful to remain. It was built in the mid or late 19th century to drain a claypit at the brickworks nearby and had ceased to work by 1923. It has stood derelict for at least 60 years but still retains virtually all its gear. The tower is very short, being only some 12 feet high. The cap frame is simple and probably never had a roof. The iron windshaft has a crank connected directly to the up and down upright shaft, which is more correctly a 'connecting rod'. The cap was winded by a large vane and the sails, mounted on a small cross, would have probably been of the spring type. The upright shaft connects through a universal joint to a small lift pump of iron set in the base of the tower. How the mill operated is now impossible to establish but as it is a fixed structure must have involved extensive temporary leats and culverts as the pit covers a large area. The mill appears to be safe from demolition and will probably remain in its present state for many years, unless any restoration is embarked upon, that is.

115. Sutton St. James TF389191 Ives Cross Mill 1972, 1983 int.

Dated 'W.E.R.1828', this small mill worked by wind until about 1923 and then continued by engine with the cap removed and a simple flat roof on the curb. In this form it probably worked until the 1950's or even into the 60's and may have produced flour for the associated bakery until quite late. It is now disused and following the collapse of part of the roof is becoming very derelict internally which is a shame as it is one of the most complete mills in the county. It was driven by four single sided patent sails mounted on stocks in a poll end. When the sails were removed the stocks were made into four large gate posts to the mill yard which still survive. Many of the floor beams and joists appear to be re-used, one having been a shaft at one time and the dust floor beams having a curve and many redundant mortices. Several common sail whips can also be seen. As no mill is shown here on the 1824 O.S. map, these pieces may have come from elsewhere.

There are three pairs of stones, one of grey and two of French. One of the pairs of French stones has a reciprocating sieve (or 'jumper') fed directly by the spout and driven by the spindle to produce a wheatmeal flour from the wholemeal. The great spur wheel is of iron and drives through mortice nuts. The engine drive also engages by means of a mortice nut on the spur wheel, with bevel wheels under the ground floor leading to an external pulley, which is unusually of wooden construction. As a steady speed could be maintained by the engine the governor was dispensed with. An ancillary drive was taken from an iron tooth ring under the spur wheel but the shafts and machines which it once drove (probably a flour dresser and oat roller) have gone. The upright shaft is of iron with a wooden upper section as is often the case in the county and has an iron wallower. The sackhoist is driven by a wooden ring under the wallower and the top bearing is mounted on one of the old sheer-trees, which also formed the ridge of the roof. All the floors are now ruinous although the machinery has remained in good condition.

116. Swaby TF380769 1978, 1985 int.

This tower mill was unusual in being hand-winded until the end of its working life. It was built in 1812 on former common land, went out of use in the 1910's and after some gale damage was dismantled in 1923. A wheel at the rear of the cap was used in winding by endless rope or chain. The four patent sails drove two pairs of grey and one pair of French stones. It was an empty shell by 1942 and now stands derelict with the top few courses of the tower missing.

117. Swineshead TF229415 North End 1977, 1985 int.

Described as being 'newly erected upon an old site' in 1821, this small tower mill worked until the early 1930's, latterly with no fantail, being hand-winded when required. The sails were blown off c.1931 after the curb distorted, causing the cap to jam. The cap had gone by the 1950's and it was allowed to become very derelict, the floors having collapsed by the early 1980's. From this absolute nadir it has been rescued in the nick of time by mill enthusiast David Bent, assisted by his father Stanley. They acquired the mill in 1983 and have embarked upon a full restoration, using parts salvaged from other mills as what remained of the old gear, being wooden, was beyond repair. The adjacent storage building is being converted into living accommodation and at the time of writing the tower has a temporary conical roof and is undergoing repair. The project is likely to take many years and deserves every encouragement. When finished it should have little difficulty in earning its keep as it is on the perimeter of the large village and near to a busy main road. There are two pairs of stones, one French and one grey, with a wooden great spur wheel and upright shaft, once driven by four single sided patent sails mounted on a cross.

118. Toynton All Saints TF392640 1977, 1985

Another very small tower mill, this replaced a post mill in the early 19th century. It was winded by wheel and chain until 1905, when an enormous fantail was added to the little cap, dwarfing it. It worked until the early 1930's and then became derelict. The cap was taken off in the 1950's leaving the tower intact but disused. In 1978 the remaining gear (two pairs of stones, upright shaft with wallower and great spur wheel, stone nuts, spindles and tentering gear) was taken out and fitted to Lincoln mill, where it may now be seen at work. The empty tower was converted into a house in the early 1980's. The sails were spring shuttered and were carried on a poll end, very unusual in this part of the county.

119. Trusthorpe TF513840 1978

This belongs to that rare breed, the moved tower mill. It was erected to replace a post mill in 1880-1 and originally stood at Newland, near Hull. Mr. Charles Foster bought it, demolished it and shipped everything but the bricks around to Mablethorpe where it was offloaded and incorporated into a new tower. Because the old post mill had been used by mariners as a landmark, the government paid Mr. Foster to retain it for a few years so that they would become accustomed to the new mill. In fact the post mill survived, in ever increasing dilapidation, until 1901. The new tower mill had eight floors and was very tall. It worked until 1935, latterly with only two sails, when it was pulled down and converted into a house, the stump being three storeys high. There were four double sided patent sails driving four pairs of stones on the fourth floor. It managed to break two crosses during its short career.

120. Waddingham SK981961 Anderson's Mill 1978

This tower mill was rebuilt in the early 19th century and appears to incorporate the roundhouse wall of a post mill or part of an earlier tower mill. It worked until the 1910's by wind after which it was engine driven until 1946. The tower is now disused and contains later milling machinery together with the upper wooden part of the upright shaft. There were four patent sails.

121. Waddington SK974634 Worsdell's Mill 1978 int.

Built in 1820, this replaced a post mill. It worked until c.1908 and then was left to become derelict. The two remaining sails were removed in 1927 and the upper part of the tower was pulled down early in the war because of its proximity to an airfield. It now stands disused as a derelict shell. There were four patent sails driving three pairs of stones, two grey and one French.

122. Wainfleet All Saints TF495586 Salem Bridge Mill 1977, 1985

This tower mill was built c.1820 and from its similarity to Alford mill could have been by the same millwright, namely Oxley of Alford. It worked until c.1920 and was then bought by Batemans, the brewers, who dismantled it and used the premises as part of their brewery. The tower now has a crenellated top and a 'beer bottle' weathervane. Batemans now use the windmill as their trademark, although it has sprouted four sails in the middle of the tower! There were five patent sails which probably drove four pairs of stones.

123. Wainfleet St. Mary TF490582 Key's Toft 1977

Built in the early 19th century this tower mill worked until 1947 when a sail was lost. The mill was dismantled in 1949 and two sails later found their way on to

Heckington mill. It was gutted in the late 1960's and is now house converted. There were four patent sails driving three pairs of stones, two grey and one French.

124. Waltham TA259033 1978, 1983, 1985 int.

This tall, slender tower mill was built in 1880 by John Saunderson, the Louth millwright on the site of a post mill that had been blown down in December 1873. Unusually for such a case the new mill did not appear immediately as its construction did not commence until 1879, slightly before the construction of the almost identical mill at Binbrook (now demolished). The reason is probably that Saunderson built the mill for himself and subsequently let it to tenant millers, a not uncommon system adopted by the more affluent and entrepreneurial millwrights of the 19th century. He therefore chose a known mill site for his new mill instead of a fresh site which may have been unsuitable. It worked until 1962 by wind, one of the last to do so in the country, and continued to be driven by electricity until 1967. By then a Waltham Windmill Preservation Society had been formed and repairs were carried out to the cap and fantail by Thompsons. In the mid 1970's one of the four remaining sails was damaged, causing them all to be removed for safety. Cleethorpes District Council bought the mill and have embarked upon a thorough restoration, putting the mill into working order and developing the site as 'Waltham Windmill Centre' with various craft workshops and a restaurant in addition to the mill which is open to the public, who may also purchase flour made at the mill. The restoration has been carried out mainly by Thompsons of Alford, but the interior has been repaired by unemployed young people under a 'job creation scheme' funded by the Government.

Waltham Mill was built with six double sided patent sails but these were cut down to single sided sails in the 1920's, this being said to improve the performance in light winds, in addition to lightening the dead weight of the sails. It was originally built 'to a price' for although the machinery is to Saunderson's usual high standard, the cap frame and floors incorporate much second-hand timber. The almost universal reefing stage has also been deleted, necessitating an extremely long striking chain.

The ground floor is raised, with a loading platform and has the engine drive (from a large Crossley engine) entering just under the ceiling. A combined roller and crushing mill could be driven by the shaft above by belt. The first floor is the spout floor and in the ceiling can be seen the mill's unique engine drive. A secondary upright shaft comes up from bevel wheels below the floor to an iron spur wheel and mortice stone nuts driving two pairs of stones underdrift through 1:1 ratio. The huge stone nuts come as something of a surprise. One governor controls these stones while another controls the other two pairs which are overdriven in the usual manner. There are two pairs of French and two pairs of grey stones, one of each being overdriven and underdriven. The French runner stones are both dated, one '1847 George Maris' and the other '1857. Stapleton' although this stone is fitted with Clarke & Dunhams' patent stone balance weights, dated 1859. Being older than the mill they are obviously second-hand. The engine drive shaft continues up to the great spur wheel, which it engages with a normal-sized stone nut. By this means it is possible to drive all four pairs of stones by wind, or two by wind and two by power if the nut is disengaged. Whether this last option was used in practice is unlikely, in my opinion.

The third floor is the bin floor, now unfortunately gutted, as is the fourth floor. The fifth floor is completely empty and the curb holding-down bolts are accessible at this level. The sixth floor is the very cramped dust floor giving access to the cap. The wallower and upright shaft are of iron, with an iron sackhoist with endless chain. The cap sheertrees are of oak and appear to have been adapted from a smaller curb as the centring wheels have been moved further out. The brakewheel is of iron with an iron brake; the whole of the principal machinery is identical to that at Sibsey, also built by Saunderson.

The sails contain only seven bays and being only single sided appear rather small on such a big mill. The scale is deceptive however for the mill is powerful and is well winded, being in open and flat countryside. It is close to an aerodrome and had a narrow escape when a party of RAF personnel arrived at the mill during the war and told the miller they had come to demolish his mill as it was a hazard to aircraft. Fortunately for succeeding generations the miller told them in no uncertain terms to get off the premises, thus sparing the mill from the fate which befell so many others during the war.

125. Welbourne SK974535 1978

Built in 1833 for Henry Minnitt this tower mill replaced a post mill, which was offered for sale for removal to another site. By 1845 a steam mill accompanied it and work continued until early this century when it was partly demolished. The two storeyed stump remains, built into the adjoining steam mill building and is used as a store. There were four patent sails.

126. Wellingore SK984570 1977

This tower mill bears the date 1854 but in this case the datestone only applies to upper five storeys. These were added to the lower two floors of an 18th century tower mill which had four pairs of stones and was already quite a large mill. The junction was disguised by a stage and is given away by a slight change in the batter; the older part was also rendered over to smarten it up. In its rebuilt form the mill again worked four pairs of stones, driven by six patent sails. Work finished by wind in the late 1930's with two sails. The cap had been removed by 1945 and all the wind powered gear was removed for scrap. All that remained in 1977 were the floors and an engine-driven hurst on the ground floor. The mill is disused and derelict. It was the subject of a planning application for house conversion in 1985 and is likely to be preserved in this form.

127. West Butterwick (H) SE836066 1978 int.

This tower mill, on the bank of the Trent, was described as being 'newly erected' in 1824, when it had four roller reefing sails, driving three pairs of stones. It later acquired patent sails and in this form continued to work until the early 1940's, finally halted by gale damage. It became derelict and lost its cap and machinery. Some gear is thought to have survived until the late 1960's but in 1978 only the wooden upright shaft remained. The tower has a crude flat roof and is derelict. It is likely to be house converted eventually.

128. Whaplode TF308123 Shepeau Stow 1977, 1978, 1983

There was a tower mill on this site with two pairs of stones in 1800 and in 1837 it was described as being 'old-established'. It may well be an eighteenth century mill although the upper part of the tower looks newer than the bottom to me. The machinery is principally of wood however, with a clasp arm great spur wheel. Work ceased in the early 1920's when a sail was lost but continued with an engine to a hurst for many years. The cap was off by 1935 and in the absence of a proper roof it has become a ruin, with most of the floors collapsed. Power came from four patent sails carried on stocks and two pairs of stones were driven, one French and one grey, together with a further pair of grey stones on a ground floor hurst. Most of the lower machinery is believed to remain, albeit in very poor condition.

129. Wildmore TF241533 Haven Bank 1977 int.

Documentary records for the Wildmore mills are somewhat confused as there were also tower mills at Scrub Hill and New York, both within two miles of Haven Bank mill. It probably dates from the early 1800's and all three were standing by 1824. It was raised by one floor in 1886 but is still little more than 30 feet high to the curb. The cap was of a more 'flared' variety than usual and probably indicates that the mill was older than most of the local mills. It ceased work in the 1930's and by 1947 the sails were off. The cap and windshaft were later removed and the mill now stands derelict. It had four single sided patent sails and drove two pairs of stones, one French and one grey. These remain, as do the wooden upright shaft and clasp arm great spur wheel.

130. Woodhall Spa TF176626 Kirkstead Mill 1977

This tower mill was built to replace a post mill in the late 19th century, possibly as late as the 1880's, with an integral steam engine and four pairs of stones. In 1887 however, it caught fire and was gutted, the machinery being sold off the following year including a 'four-horned cross'. It was reinstated as an engine powered mill and worked until the 1930's at least. It was later almost completely demolished and only the single storeyed stump remains, converted into a garage.

131. Woolsthorpe SK836363 Stenwith 1978 int.

This tower mill is something of an enigma. It is not marked on the 1824 O.S. map and although shown on the 1908 map appears to have been disused by this time. What remains is the lower two storeys of a red brick tower mill, probably of early 19th century date. It is crudely roofed over and is used as a store.

132. Wragby TF131778 1977, 1983 int.

This tall tower mill was built in 1831 by the millwright Ingledew. It worked by wind until 1903 when an oil engine took over. It was modernised subsequently, with the old gearing removed. It remains in the corn trade although the tower is only used as a store now. It had six sails which drove four pairs of stones on the third floor and the upper stone spindle glut box bearings survive in place. The only other wind-driven gear to remain is part of the sackhoist, which used an endless chain. The cap has been replaced by a low concrete dome which is supported by the old oak sheertrees. There is a large hurst frame on the spacious ground floor which formerly contained two pairs of stones while a large grain cleaner by E.R.&F.Turner of Ipswich is on an upper floor.

133. Wrangle TF443516 Toft Mill 1977 int., 1985

This tower mill, or its predecessor, is first shown on the 1824 O.S. map. It was dismantled c.1922 and converted to an engine-driven mill. No original machinery remained but there was a ground floor hurst with one pair of stones and a mixer. It had four patent sails. It now stands abandoned and derelict.

134. Wrangle TF439511 Wrangle Mill 1977, 1985

This tower mill is not shown on the 1824 O.S. map but probably dates from around that time. It has been raised by a floor and worked by wind until the 1930's. It was later dismantled and modernised, an electric hammer mill and mixer being in use in 1977. There were four patent sails.

135. Wrawby (H) TA026087 1978, 1985 int.

The sole survivor of the multitude of post mills once to be found in the county, this was originally built in the mid-late 18th century as an open trestle mill, although the site may well have been previously occupied by a mill. The roundhouse, of the roofless 'Midland' type was erected in the early 19th century and in this form the mill worked until 1940 by wind, and until the late 40's by engine in an adjacent power mill that had been set up in 1914. The mill was then allowed to fall into decay, which it did with almost unseemly haste. By 1961 it was a wreck and permission was sought to demolish it by the owner. Happily though, it was rescued and entirely rebuilt, using some original machinery and the post, largely by volunteers led by Jon Sass and Edward Travis between 1962 and 1965. Using two second-hand sails from Halton Holegate mill and shutters from Maud Foster mill, Boston, flour was made once more in September 1965. Subsequently the other two sails were fitted and further internal work was carried out by Thompsons of Alford. The mill was worked on open days, wind permitting, and flour was sold to visitors. Unfortunately it suffered and attack from the windmill's worst enemy, a tailwind, in 1978. This allowed the sails to rotate backwards, smashing them and causing the tail of the windshaft to come out of the bearing, causing some internal damage. It was repaired, again by Thompsons, and the mill is once again in full working order and open to the public.

It originally had four common sails, then gained two spring sails, ending up with a full set of spring sails, the last original set being converted from patent sails off a mill at Laceby. Winding is by tailpole and winch, with a lever to raise the steps clear of the ground. The body, which like the trestle is very heavily timbered in oak, is steadied by six rollers which run on a curb on the roundhouse wall.

The wooden windshaft was converted from a poll end by fitting an iron cross to the front end. The brake wheel is clasp arm with an iron tooth ring and drives a pair of 4ft. 6in. French stones, the runner being dated 1846, by George Maris of Hull. The tail wheel, now clasp arm, was originally compass arm and had been used as a brake wheel, probably from another local mill. It also has an iron tooth ring and drives a pair of 4ft. grey stones. There is a sackhoist above, driven by friction from the rim of the tail wheel, and a small wire machine which can be driven by belt from the rim of the tail wheel or by an electric motor. The lower floor is quite spacious and is liberally sprinkled with flour dust, creating the pleasing impression of a working mill.

136. Wyberton TF306428 1978

Built in the early 19th century, this tower mill worked until the 1910's. It was then abandoned and by 1935 had been reduced to a short thatched stump. In 1978 only the derelict wall of the lower storey remained. The mill was once worked by John Pocklington (of Heckington) and it is said that the four sails from here were put on Heckington mill when work finished at Wyberton.

Some Bygone Mills

The following windmills have all disappeared since the 1930's, usually completely, but occasionally leaving scant remains. These are noted where the author has personal knowledge of them but there may well be other such remains waiting to be discovered. While I have tried to include all the mills to have stood since about 1930 there may well be gaps so this list should not be taken as being exhaustive.

Alford TF453758 Myer's Mill. Tall six sail tower mill, built 1827; raised 1889; ceased work 1949, gutted 1950's, tower demolished 1978.

Bardney TF120696 Tall six sail tower mill; built 1830; demolished 1946.

Barlings TF064764 Langworth. Smock mill, moved from Market Rasen in early 19th century; ceased work in 1930's, demolished in 1950's or 60's.

Barrow Upon Humber (H) TA 066213 Tall tower mill, demolished early 1970's.

Barton Upon Humber (H) TA037211 Caistor Road. Large four sail mill, working until late 1930's, dismantled in 1960's, tower demolished between 1978 and 1983.

Barton Upon Humber (H) TA025219 Milson's Mill. Large four sail tower mill; sails removed 1878; power driven until 1920, demoliished 1934.

Barton Upon Humber (H) TA028231 Sisson's Mill, Waterside. A whiting mill, tower demolished 1946.

Bicker TF227374 A house converted tower in 1934, burnt out in 1936 and demolished.

Binbrook TF209938 Tall six sail tower mill, built 1879, ceased work in 1938 and pulled down early in the war.

Boston TF313437 Day's Mill. Tower standing in 1953 but gone by late 1970's.

Boston TF334449 Thompson's Mill, Skirbeck. Tall tower mill; cap taken off 1882 and put on a new pumping mill at Sleaford. Tower survived into 1950's but gone by late 1970's.

Carlton-le-Moorland SK897585 Open trestle post mill; collapsed 1935.

Carrington TF311554 Small tower mill; tower survived into 1950's but gone by early 70's.

Coleby SK989603 Coleby Heath. Tall six sail tower mill; pulled down in 1942 due to proximity to airfield; stump remained in mid 1950's but gone by early 1970's.

Coningsby TF224579 Five sail tower mill, built 1826; demolished in 1970 when still complete for a road widening scheme. A sad loss.

Crowle (H) SE776132 Mill Road. One of a group of two tower mills and a post mill. It went in the 1950's or 60's. The foundations of the second tower mill were visible in the 1930's in the garden of a house.

Crowle (H) SE772123 Godnow Road. Tower mill; a shell in the 1950's but gone by the late 1970's.

Deeping St. James TF156099 Very stoutly built stone tower mill, demolished in 1960's.

Donington TF204355 Rippon's Mill. Five sail tower mill; stump pulled down in early 1960's.

Foston SK860423 Large post mill with 'midland' roundhouse; built c.1700, moved c.1760, ceased work 1928, demolished 1966.

Friskney TF466547 Kitching's Mill. Tower mill, built 1824; tower survived in 1950's, gone by early 1970's.

Friskney TF481554 Toft Mill. Open trestle mill, dated 1730. Worked until early 1930's, blown down 1939.

Frithville TF320505 Tower mill; stump remained in 1930's, gone by early 1970's.

Gainsborough SK806907 Union Mill. Tall five sail oil mill; tower remained in 1920's but gone by 1953. In 1978 parts of the foundations were visible.

Gedney TF464294 Gedney Drove End. Small tower mill, derelict in 1930's, gone by 1953.

Gosberton TF204297 Small tower mill; derelict in 1950's, gone by late 1970's.

Grimsby (H) TA267071 Scartho. Large five sail tower mill, built in 1869; derelict in 1950's, gone by 1978.

Halton Holegate TF414646 Small tower mill, dated 1814; ceased work in late 1940's; dismantled c.1962-3, demolished in mid 1960's. Two sails put on Wrawby mill.

Holbeach TF364240 Damgate Mill. Tower mill, dated 1816, raised 1867, ceased work 1944, demolished in 1960's. In 1982 the foundations and several millstones were visible.

Holbeach TF359224 Tindall's Mill. Large eight sail tower mill, built in 1828. Three storeyed base remained in 1953, incorporated into modern power mill. By late 1970's had gone, modern mill buildings on site.

Horsington TF196695 Tower mill; base remained in 1953, gone by 1977.

Ingham SK957832 Tower mill; tower stood in 1953, gone by 1977.

Keadby with Althorpe (H) SE836111 Tower mill; shell stood in 1953; gone by 1978.

Kettlethorpe SK834757 Laughterton. Post mill with roundhouse; dated 1787, ceased work by wind late 1930's, by engine 1950. Demolished 1951 when some parts were taken to Heapham Mill for preservation. Whether or not they still remain is not known to the author. In 1978 the lower part of the roundhouse walling remained.

Kexby SK872853 Sometimes known as 'Willingham Mill'. Four sail tower mill, derelict in 1930's, gone by 1953.

Kexby SK871860 Britannia Flour Mills. Large tower mill, built 1856 on site of a 'subscription mill' (sometimes known as 'Upton mill'). Worked by wind until late 1930's then power driven. Cap remained with fantail until demolition, c.1972-3.

Lincoln SK972724 Mill Road. Tower mill; tower remained in 1930's, gone by 1953.

Metheringham TF 122643 Sots Hole. Tower mill, base used as house in 1932, demolished c.1959-60.

Normanby by Spital SK994878 Tower mill, demolished 1965. In 1978 several millstones remained.

North Hykeham SK934663 Hykeham Moor. Post mill with roundhouse; dated 1756, ceased work in the Great War; collapsed late 1930's and cleared away.

North Somercoates TF416965 Tower mill, shell stood in 1953, gone by 1978.

Old Leake TF401523 Leake Commonside, Gosling's Mill. Tower mill, demolished c.1970.

Owston Ferry (H) SE817004 Tower mill, working until 1937 when accidentally set on fire and burnt out. Demolished shortly afterwards.

Pinchbeck TF202262 Horse and Jockey Mill. Small tower mill, derelict in late 1940's, gone by 1977.

Potter Hanworth TF054664 Tower mill, derelict in 1930's, gone by 1953.

Ropsley and Humby TF005339 Humby Mill. Old stone tower mill, disused since 1880's. Tower remained in 1930's; in 1977 only fragments of wall remained.

Saxby All Saints (H) SE994177 Tower mill; tower demolished in 1960's; windshaft and cross preserved at Skidby.

Scawby (H) SE987067 Bratley's Mill, Mill Place, Brigg. Large five sail tower mill converted to steam power, demolished 1930.

Scopwick TF094578 Kirkby Green. Post mill with 'midland' type roundhouse; dated 1830, moved from Digby c.1865, ceased work 1909, collapsed 1935. Parts of the trestle and the post are said to remain near the site.

South Killingholme (H) TA152153 Post mill with 'midland' type roundhouse; dated 1716, ceased work c.1930, demolished 1935; roundhouse remained later but gone by 1978.

South Kyme TF169498 Tower mill, standing in 1953, gone by early 1970's.

South Willingham TF182824 Tower mill, working until late 1930's, demolished 1958.

South Witham SK924192 Old tower mill, dated 1793; possibly raised later; ceased work c.1920, derelict in 1930's. In 1977 fragments of the walls remained; the datestone and two French stones were preserved in the garden of the adjacent house.

Spalding TF234211 Little London. Narrow tower mill; ceased work 1944, demolished 1948.

Swineshead TF240404 Houlder's Mill. Tower mill; worked until late 1930's; tower remained in 1950's, gone by early 1970's.

Theddlethorpe St. Helen TF472873 Tower mill, built 1833; derelict in 1953; gone by 1978. The foundations are said to be visible.

Worlaby (H) TH001131 Small tower mill; derelict in 1930's, demolished by 1953. In 1978 the foundations were visible.

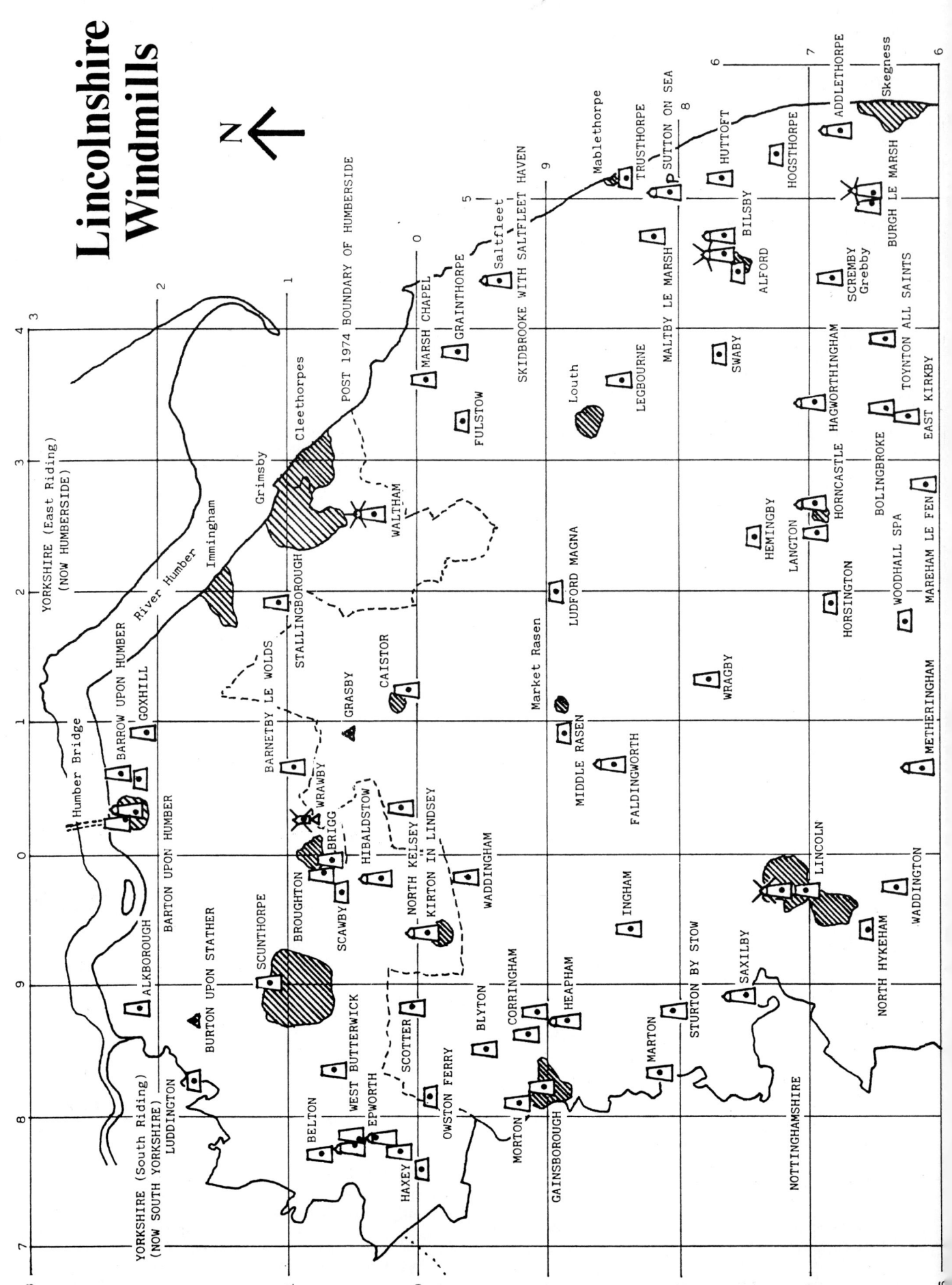

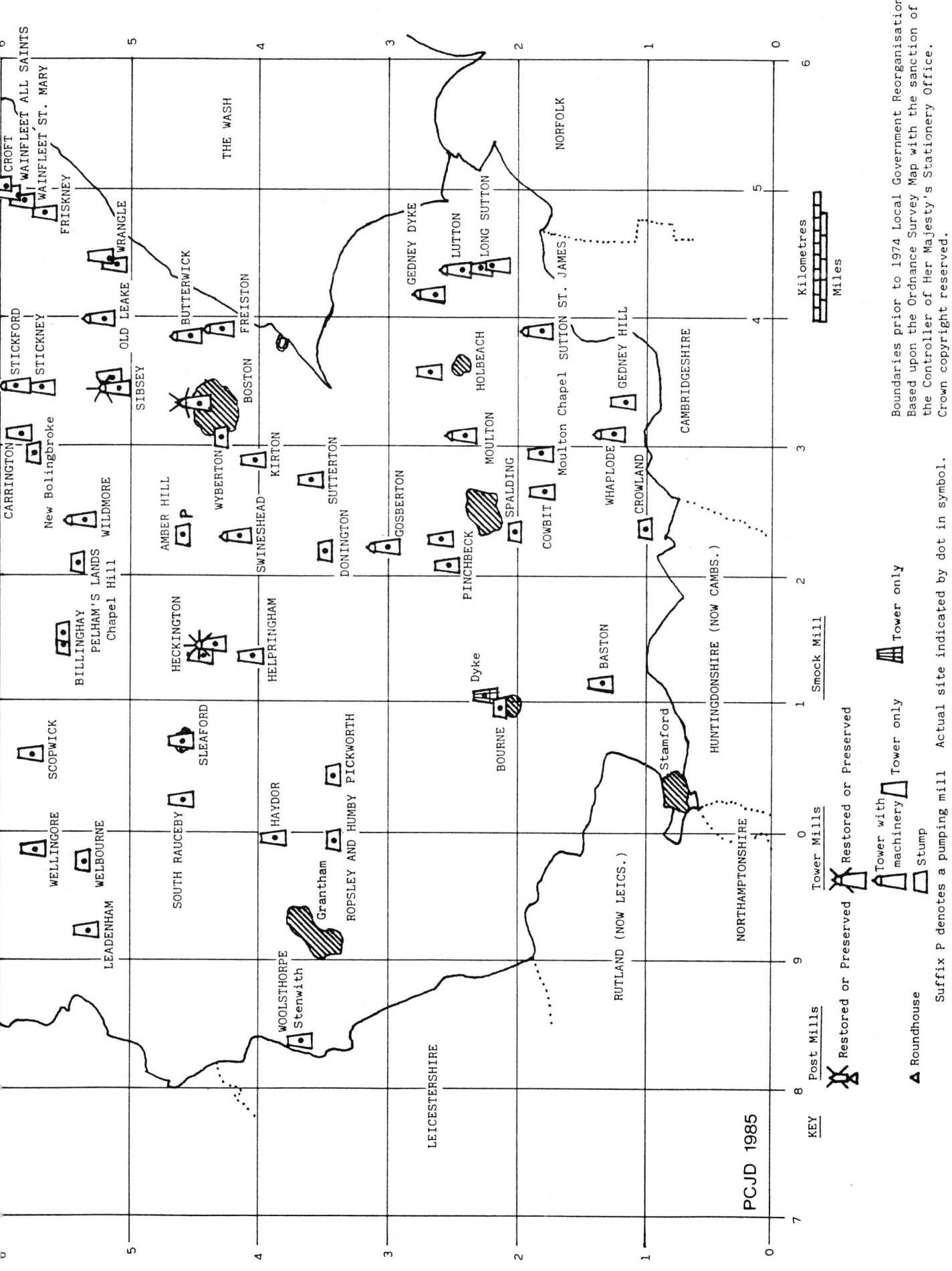

Addlethorpe: 1973

Alford: Grain cleaner, 1985

Alford: Hoyle's Mill, 1973

Alford: Stone floor, 1985

Alford: Sackhoist Drive, Wallower & Brakewheel, 1985

Alford: Station Mill, 1978

Alford: Jim Davies of R. Thompson & Son at their workshop in Parsons Lane, 1985

Amber Hill: 1978

Alford: R. Thompson & Son's workshop Brakewheel for Sneinton Mill, Nottingham under construction, 1985

Barnetby le Wold: 1978

Alkborough: 1983

Barrow upon Humber: Barrow Haven, 1978

Barrow upon Humber: Pearson's Mill, 1978

Barton upon Humber: Market Place, 1983 Great Spur Wheel

Barton upon Humber: Hewson's Mill, 1978

Barton upon Humber: Market Place, 1983 Bridge Tree

Barton upon Humber: Market Place, 1985

Barton upon Humber: Market Place, 1983 Former Whiting Mill Drive

Baston: 1983

Billinghay: West Mill, 1978

Bilsby: 1985

Belton: 1985

Blyton: 1978

Billinghay: East Mill, 1977

Bolingbroke: Postcard, c.1930

Boston: Maud Foster Mill, 1971

Bolingbroke: Old Bolingbroke, 1978

Boston: Maud Foster Mill, Stone floor, 1982

Boston: Maud Foster Mill, dressed overall in the 1930s (Photographer unknown)

Boston: Maud Foster Mill — Governor, 1982

Broughton: Castlethorpe Mill, 1978

Bourne: 1971

Bourne: Dyke Mill, 1971

Burgh le Marsh: Dobson's Mill, 1977

Brigg: Bell's Mill, 1978

Burgh le Marsh: Fantail gearing and brake lever, 1985

Burgh le Marsh: Oat crusher and engine drive, 1985

Butterwick: 1977

Burgh le Marsh: Hanson's Mill, 1977

Butterwick: Governor and tentering gear, 1977

Burton upon Stather: 1978

Caistor: Wright's Mill, 1978

Carrington: Watkinson's Mill, New Bolingbroke, 1973

Corringham: West Mill (Winter's), 1978

Carrington: Rundle's Mill, New Bolingbroke, 1973

Cowbit: 1972

Corringham: East Mill, 1978

Croft: 1934, H. E. S. Simmons

41

Croft: 1977

East Kirkby: 1973

Crowland: 1971

Epworth: Maw's Mill, 1985

Epworth: Brook's Mill, 1985

Donington: 1977

Epworth: Thompson's Mill, 1978

Friskney: Hoyle's Mill, 1977

Faldingworth: 1985

Fulstow: 1978

Freiston: 1977

Gainsborough: Spital Hill, 1978

Gedney Dyke: 1977

Goxhill: 1978

Gedney Hill: 1977

Grainthorpe: 1978

Gosberton: Risegate Mill, 1977

Grasby: 1978

Hagworthingham:
F. Girling, 1929

Haxey: 1978

Hagworthingham: 1978

Haydor:
Oasby Mill,
1977

Heapham: 1978

Haxey: 1978

Heckington: Pocklington's Mill c.1930 (Photographer unknown)

Heckington: 'Lag' Governor, 1985

Heckington: Pocklington's Mill, 1982

Heckington: Mowbray's Mill, Sleaford Road, 1985

Heckington: Sackhoist, 1985

Helpringham: 1985

46

Hemingby: 1977

Hogsthorpe: 1982

Hibaldstow: 1978

Holbeach: Penny Hill, 1972

Hibaldstow: Great spur wheel, windmill, 1978

Horncastle: postcard c1900

47

Horncastle: 1982

Ingham: 1978

Kirton: Kirton End, 1977

Horsington: 1982

Kirton in Lindsey: postcard c1930

Huttoft: 1982

Kirton in Lindsey: 1978

Legbourne: 1978

Langton: 1977

Lincoln: Ellis' Mill, 1978

Leadenham: Lowfield Mill, 1977

Lincoln: Ellis' Mill, 1982

Lincoln: Le Tall's Mill, Princess Street, 1977

Long Sutton: Harrison's Mill, 1985

Long Sutton: Brunswick Mill, 1971

Luddington: 1978

Long Sutton: Brunswick Mill, 1977

Ludford Magna: 1978

Lutton: 1971

Marsh Chapel: 1978

Maltby le Marsh: 1985

Marton: 1985

Mareham le Fen: 1978

Metheringham: c.1930 (Photographer unknown)

Metheringham: 1977

Moulton: 1972

Middle Rasen: 1978

Moulton: Great spur wheel and stone nut, 1977

Morton: 1978

Moulton: Moulton Chapel, 1983

North Hykeham: 1977

Old Leake: Howsam's Mill — Great spur wheel and governor drive, 1977

North Kelsey: 1978

Owston Ferry 1978

Old Leake: Howsam's Mill, Leake Common Side, 1977

Pelham's Lands: Chapel Hill Mill, 1977

Pickworth, 1977

Ropsley with Humby: Ropsley Mill, 1977

Pinchbeck: Northgate Mill, 1977

Saxilby: 1978

Pinchbeck: Glenside Mill, 1977

Scawby: 1978

Scopwick: 1977

Scunthorpe: 1985

Scotter: 1978

Sibsey: Trader Mill, 1985

Scremby: Grebby Mill, 1985

Sibsey: Detail of finial and sail, 1985

55

Sibsey: Rhoade's Mill, 1978

Saltfleet: Grain cleaner 1983

Saltfleet: c.1900 (Photographer unknown)

Sleaford: 1985

Saltfleet: 1983

South Rauceby: 1977

Spalding: 1977

Stickford: 1985

Stallingborough: 1983

*Stickney: c.1930
Mr. C. Donnor*

*Stickford:
postcard c.1930*

Stickney: 1985

Sturton by Stow: 1985

Sutton on Sea: Lift pump, 1982

Sutterton: 1970

Sutton on Sea: 1982

Sutton St James: 1972

Sutton St James: Stone floor, 1983

Toynton All Saints: 1985

Swaby: 1985

Trusthorpe: 1978

Swineshead 1985

Toynton All Saints: 1951, G. C. Wilson

Waddingham: 1978

Waddington: 1978

Wainfleet St Mary: 1977

Wainfleet All Saints: Postcard, c1900

Waltham: 1985

Wainfleet All Saints: 1977

Welbourne: 1978

60

Wellingore: 1977

Wildmore: Haven Bank Mill, 1977

Woodhall Spa: Kirkstead Mill, 1977

West Butterwick: 1978

Whaplode: Shepeau Stow, 1983

Woolsthorpe: Stenwith Mill, 1978

Wragby: 1977

Wrawby: 1978

Wrangle: Toft Mill, 1977

Wrawby: Tailwheel and stones, 1985

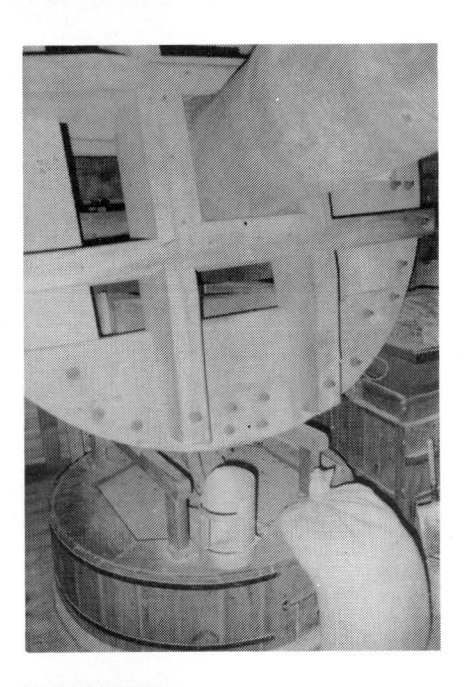

Wrangle: 1977

Wrawby: Tail governor, 1985

Wyberton: 1978

North Hykeham: The Old Postmill at Hykeham Moor, postcard c1900

Alford: Myer's Mill (now demolished) 1978

Ropsley with Humby: Remains of Humby Mill, 1977

Barton upon Humber: Caistor Road (now demolished) 1978

South Witham: Fragments of Tower, 1977

Selected Bibliography

Brown, R.J.	'Windmills of England' (Contains potted histories of several Lincolnshire mills)	Robert Hale, 1976
Freese, Stanley	'Windmills and Millwrighting' (very good on constructional details)	David & Charles, 1971
Freese, Stanley, and Hopkins, Thurston	'In Search of English Windmills' (a 'travelogue' book with many references to Lincolnshire mills)	Cecil Palmer, 1931
Lincoln Civic Trust	'Ellis' Windmill'	1982
Lincolnshire Mills Group	'The Windmill at Burgh le Marsh'	1984
Pocklington, A.R.	'Heckington Windmill'	Lincolnshire County Council 1984
Vince, John	'Discovering Windmills' (a good introduction to windmills)	Shire Publications, 1984
Wailes, Rex	'The English Windmill' (standard work on the subject with excellent chapter on Sibsey mill)	Routledge & Kegan Paul, 1954
Wailes, Rex	Lincolnshire Windmills Part 1 — Post Mills Part 2 — Tower Mills (The only published work on Lincolnshire Windmills)	Transactions of the Newcomen Society Volume 28, 1951-3 Volume 29, 1953-5
Anon.	'Wrawby Post Mill'	1970

This book forms part of the County Windmills Series of Contemporary Surveys. Other volumes are:

'Windmills in Hertfordshire'   1974 (Out of print, revised edition due 1986)
'Windmills in Bedfordshire'   1975 (Out of print)
'Windmills in Cambridgeshire'   1975 (Out of print)
'Windmills in Surrey and Greater London'   1976 (Out of print)
'Windmills in Buckinghamshire and Oxfordshire'   1976 (Out of print)
'Windmills in Huntingdon and Peterborough'   1977 (Out of print)
'Drainage Windmills of the Norfolk Marshes'   1978 (Out of print)
'Windmills in Sussex'   1980
'Corn Windmills in Norfolk'   1982

The above are by Arthur C. Smith and are published by Stevenage Museum.

'Windmills in Warwickshire'   1977 (Out of print)
by Wilfred A. Seaby and Arthur C. Smith, published by Warwickshire Museum.

'Windmills in Staffordshire'   1980
by Wilfred A. Seaby & Arthur C. Smith, published by Stafford County Museum.

'Windmills in Shropshire, Hereford and Worcester'   1984
by Wilfred A. Seaby & Arthur C. Smith, published by Stevenage Museum.

'Windmills in Suffolk'   1978 (Out of print)
by Peter C.J. Dolman, published by Suffolk Mills Group.

The Wind and Watermill Section of the Society for the Protection of Ancient Buildings advises on matters concerning mills and welcomes new members.
Contact: The Secretary, S.P.A.B., 37 Spital Square, London, E1 6DY.

The Lincolnshire Mills Group caters for local mill enthusiasts and welcomes new members.
Contact: The Hon. Secretary, L.M.G., 75 Yarborough Road, Lincoln, LN1 1HS.